The Python Quick
Syntax Reference

Gregory Walters

Apress·

The Python Quick Syntax Reference

ISBN-13 (pbk): 978-1-4302-6478-1

ISBN-13 (electronic): 978-1-4302-6479-8

President and Publisher: Paul Manning
Lead Editor: Jonathan Hassell
Developmental Editor: James Markham
Technical Reviewer: Michael Winiberg
Editorial Board: Steve Anglin, Mark Beckner, Ewan Buckingham, Gary Cornell, Louise Corrigan, Jim DeWolf, Jonathan Gennick, Jonathan Hassell, Robert Hutchinson, Michelle Lowman, James Markham, Matthew Moodie, Jeff Olson, Jeffrey Pepper, Douglas Pundick, Ben Renow-Clarke, Dominic Shakeshaft, Gwenan Spearing, Matt Wade, Steve Weiss
Coordinating Editor: Jill Balzano
Copy Editor: Laura Lawrie
Compositor: SPi Global
Indexer: SPi Global
Artist: SPi Global
Cover Designer: Anna Ishchenko

Distributed to the book trade worldwide by Springer Science+Business Media New York, 233 Spring Street, 6th Floor, New York, NY 10013. Phone 1-800-SPRINGER, fax (201) 348-4505, e-mail orders-ny@springer-sbm.com, or visit www.springeronline.com. Apress Media, LLC is a California LLC and the sole member (owner) is Springer Science + Business Media Finance Inc (SSBM Finance Inc). SSBM Finance Inc is a Delaware corporation.

For information on translations, please e-mail rights@apress.com, or visit www.apress.com.

Apress and friends of ED books may be purchased in bulk for academic, corporate, or promotional use. eBook versions and licenses are also available for most titles. For more information, reference our Special Bulk Sales–eBook Licensing web page at www.apress.com/bulk-sales.

Any source code or other supplementary materials referenced by the author in this text is available to readers at www.apress.com. For detailed information about how to locate your book's source code, go to www.apress.com/source-code/.

*This book is dedicated to Carol, Douglas, Kirsti, Andrew and Trey . . .
My family and my world.*

Contents at a Glance

Contents

About the Author

Gregory Walters has been developing software solutions since 1972, back in the days before personal computers. Since then, he has written software in Visual Basic, Python, Cobol, Fortran, Modula-2, Modula-3, C, Pascal, VB.NET, and, most recently, in Basic4Android. He is currently working as an author writing monthly articles on Python programming for Full Circle magazine and as a consultant in Aurora, Colorado. In his spare time, he enjoys spending time with his wife, children, grandson, and dogs hiking, cooking, and playing music.

About the Technical Reviewer

Michael Winiberg received a B.Sc. in Colour Chemistry from Leeds, and he has been a developer all of his working life. He has written for ICL1900 series mainframes, Elliot "mini" computers and KDF9, through Z80, Motorola 68K, and Inmos Transputer to the current range of Intel x86 CPUsFrom implementing operating systems in assembler, a payroll written in Algol-60, or working on a precursor to GPS through to a multiuser WAN based travel reservation system in C++ with an AJAX/Java web front-end, he has had an incredibly interesting and varied career. He is currently working on Python and SQL Server projects. He has built multisite heterogenous networks, with monitoring and backup based on Linux, and IP telephony call-centers. He also has a keen interest in desktop and ebook publishing and technical writing.

He has been a senior manager and project leader, following a career as a consultant. He has long-term links to the financial industry, and recently maintained and developed for a trading floor in the City of London. His two current projects are in SQL Server/Windows Server, and Linux/Python.

His other interests include sailing, reading, walking, and playing the pipe organ. His son has just completed his Ph.D. in chemistry at Leeds. And his cat just loves chasing the mouse pointer across the screen, scattering everything off the desk . . .

Acknowledgments

First, I have to thank my wonderful wife for believing in me and for supporting me each and every day when I'm frustrated and banging my head on the keyboard at 3 am or in the late nights.

Second, I want to thank Ronnie Tucker at Full Circle magazine. Ronnie took a chance on me years ago as a fledgling author, allowing me to get started in this industry and to hone my skills on the wonderful readers of Full Circle. Thanks to you all!

Next, I want to thank the folks at Apress, with whom I've been working on this book on a daily basis: James Markham, Jill Balzano, Michael Winiberg, and Jonathan Hassell. Without their help, I would be floundering in a sea of words that make no sense. Thanks go out to all of the others who have worked and helped on this book.

Finally, I'd like to thank my children Douglas, Kirsti, and Andrew, my grandson Trey, friends, and church family (not mutually exclusive by the way) for all their longtime kindness, love, and support.

Introduction

One of the best things that Python offers is an extensive standard library that offers a wide range of included features that range from network functionality, database handling, and XML processing all the way to zip file processing. There are hundreds of additional libraries that extend the abilities of Python.

The current versions of Python that are available at this writing are 2.7 and 3.2.5. The reason for this is that version 3.x is NOT completely backward compatible to the earlier versions, and with the wealth of existing code and libraries that are currently being used on a daily basis, both versions are available. You can find these versions at www.python.org for the Windows, Linux/Unix, and Mac OS X operating systems. If you are running Linux, you can check your normal distribution, which will have a version of Python available. It might already be installed on your system. You can do a web search for versions that are available for other operating systems.

Although there are many free and for-pay IDEs (Integrated Development Editors) available for Python, all code may be written in a standard text editor and run from the command line in a standard terminal or command box. My personal preference is a free IDE named Geany, which is available for both Linux and Windows.

The goal of this book is to provide (as the name suggests) a quick guide to the Python language syntax. Sometimes, a programmer is called on to know multiple languages and the differences from one programming language to another can be just different enough to cause issues. This guide is designed to be kept not on the bookshelf but on the desk, to provide a way to quickly get answers.

You'll find chapters on data structures, keywords, strings, variables, and more. There is even a chapter on some of the more useful standard libraries that come with almost every distribution of Python.

Conventions used in this book

Almost all code presented here will be simple examples showing how to use a particular command or function and can be run in the interpreter shell. The code will look like the following, with the output or response from the shell in bold.

```
print('This is a test')
This is a test
```

If you see a line of code that starts with ">>>", that shows the prompt from the interpreter shell. Do not insert that into your code, just the part after it. If you see a line of code that starts with ". . .", that shows that the shell recognizes this is a line that should be indented. Again, do not insert the dots in your code. Just remember that you have to indent that portion of the code.

■ ■ ■

## CHAPTER 1

Hello Python

Let's review a simple Python program that will explain the use of the Python Interactive Shell along with a few tips.

Python's Interactive Shell

Once you have Python installed on your system, you can use the Interactive Shell to try simple lines of code, debug some problematic code, and even use it as a simple calculator.

In a terminal (Linux) or Command Prompt (Windows), simply type:

```
python
```

If you are running on Linux, you will see something like this:

```
Python 2.7.3 (default, Apr 10 2013, 05:09:49)
[GCC 4.7.2] on linux2
Type "help", "copyright", "credits" or "license" for more information.
>>>
```

Or if you are running on Windows, you would see something like this:

```
    Python 2.7.1 (r271:86832, Nov 27 2010, 18:30:46) [MSC v.1500 32 bit
(Intel)] on
win32
Type "help", "copyright", "credits" or "license" for more information.
>>>
```

As you can see, there is not a lot of difference in the two.

Commands

Once you see the three "right arrow" symbols (>>>), you are at the user prompt. From here you can enter commands:

```
>>> 3+23
26
>>> print "This is a test of the interactive mode"
This is a test of the interactive mode
>>> a = 3
>>> b = 4
>>> print a * b
12
>>> print a + b
7
>>> exit()
```

Multiline Statements

You can also enter multiline statements that are indented as in a *for* loop or an *if* statement (which will be discussed in a later chapter). For example:

```
>>> for i in range(0,3):
...     print i
...
0
1
2
```

When you are in multiline statements, the interpreter will automatically recognize this (by the ":" colon) and prompt you with three dots instead of three right arrows. Be sure to use spaces to indent your next line(s). To end the multiline mode, simply press "enter" on a blank line. Your multiline statement will then be evaluated (if possible) and the result will be displayed.

To exit the interactive shell, type "exit()" as shown earlier.

The Code

I know that you are "chomping at the bit" to write your first program, so we'll get started with a very simple example. Assuming that you have Python installed on your machine, fire up your favorite text editor to enter the following lines:

```
print 'Hello. I am a Python program.'
name = raw_input("What is your name? ")
print 'Hello there ' + name + '!'
```

Save this as 'hello.py' whereever you like. I'd suggest you create a subfolder of your home directory to store all your test code, like this:

```
C:\
  |-Development
              |-Tests
```

Now in a command or terminal window, change to the folder you saved the above file in and type:

```
python hello.py
```

You should see something like this:

```
greg@earth:~$ python hello.py
Hello. I am a Python program.
What is your name? Greg (The program pauses here for you to enter your name)
Hello there Greg!
```

or under Windows:

```
C:\> python hello.py
Hello. I am a Python program.
What is your name? Greg (The program pauses here for you to enter your name)
Hello there Greg!
```

Decoding the Code

Let's look at each line of the code.

```
print 'Hello. I am a Python program.'
```

The print command will output into the terminal or command prompt box whatever follows.

In this case, we are telling Python to display "Hello. I am a Python program." Notice that what we want displayed is in single quotes in our code. You can use either single or double quotes to enclose the string. However, when you want to show single quotes within a display string, you should use double quotes to enclose the entire string. If you want to display double quotes within a display string, you should use single quotes to enclose the string. We'll discuss this later in Chapter 4.

```
name = raw_input("What is your name? ")
```

3

Here we are doing two things. First, we are using the raw_input command to tell Python to display a prompt to the user (the "What is your name? " part) and then wait for the user to input something, even if it is a simple "enter" key to enter a blank input. It is important for you to include the space after the question mark and before the ending quote. This gives a cleaner look for the program, in that the ultimate user has an idea that there is something they need to do. The second thing we are doing is assigning the user's response to a variable called 'name'. We will talk more about variables in Chapter 2. For now, think of a variable as a simple box that holds something. In this case, it would hold the name of the user:

```
print 'Hello there ' + name + '!'
```

Again, we are telling Python to display a line in the terminal window, but this time we are creating the line out of three strings of text. This is called concatenation. The plus symbol ('+') is used to join the parts of the line together. So we have "Hello there" **and** the user name **and** a "!".

Comments

Comments allow us to put notes within our code. When the interpreter encounters a comment, it ignores the rest of the line. It is considered good practice to comment your code well to explain the thought process behind it. If you ever have to come back to your code after a week or so, the comments will help you remember what you were doing. It also allows other people to understand your code.

To create a comment line, simply start the comment with the hash symbol (#). The following lines are example of commented lines:

```
# This is a full line comment.
aVariable = 23 # this is an in-line comment.
```

It is important to remember that anything following the hash symbol is considered a comment. You can also use triple double quotes (""") to enclose multiline comments.

```
"""
This is an example of a multiline comment.
Everything between the sets of triple double quotes is considered a comment.
"""
```

Comments also allow us to tell the interpreter to ignore lines of code that might be giving us problems or a block of code that is incomplete.

CHAPTER 2

■ ■ ■

Variables

Variables are "slots" that we can store data in. Some languages, such as C#, Visual Basic, and others, require you to declare your variables before you use them along with the type of variable it is, for example, Integer or String. Python doesn't require you to do this. As I said in the Introduction, Python uses a scheme called "Duck Typing." This means that you don't have to declare variables before they are used and that you don't have to specify what a type variable is or will be. There is a mix of opinions on this as to whether it is a good or bad thing.

Case Sensitivity

Variables names must start with either a letter (upper- or lowercase) or an underscore character. They may not begin with a number, space, or sign character.

Everything in Python is case-sensitive: not only the keywords and functions that Python provides, but for any variables you happen to create. For example:

"Print" is not the same as "print."

Because of this, you could use the word "Print" as a variable, but not the word "print." That having been said, it isn't a good idea to use "re-cased" function names or keywords.

Proper Variable Naming

A variable name should explain what the variable is used for. If you use variable names such as "x" or "q," it doesn't tell you anything about what the variable does or is for. This is termed "self-documenting." A long time ago, it was "normal" practice to use single character variable names wherever possible. Many times it was to save memory. Although there is nothing that says you can not use single letters or some obscure variable names (and it really does save time and finger power when typing a large amount of code), it will make it very difficult for you or someone else to read and maintain your code after the fact.

Because spaces are not allowed in variable names, many people use what is called Camel Casing to make the variable names easier to understand. Camel Casing (sometimes called Pascal Casing) says that you put the first letter of each word in uppercase and all the rest in lowercase:

```
ThisIsAnExampleOfCamelCasingForVariables.
CounterVariable
ReturnedValue
```

Another alternative is to use underscores in place of spaces:

```
this_is_an_example_of_a_long_variable_name
counter_variable
returned_value
```

Either way is "acceptable." It mainly depends on what you want to use or what your work uses as a standard. As I stated earlier, it is important for you to use variable names that are "self-documenting."

Assignment

To assign a value to a variable, use the equal ("=") sign:

```
AnInteger = 3
AFloatValue = 3.14159
AString = "The time has come for all good men…"
TheList = [1,2,3,4,5]
```

You can also make multiple assignments of a single value on one line. In the following snippet, the variable 'a' is assigned to the value 1. Then the variables 'b' and 'c' are assigned to be equal to the variable 'a:'

```
>>> a = 1
>>> b = c = a
>>> print('a=%d, b=%d, c=%d') % (a,b,c)
a=1, b=1, c=1
```

Data Types

Python has five "standard" data types: numeric, string, list, tuple, and dictionary.

Numeric

Numeric data types are for storing numeric values. In Python 2.x, there are four types of numeric data, Integers (signed), Long (signed), Float (floating point numbers), and complex numbers. Booleans (0 or 1) are subtypes of integer under version 2.x. The actual range of values that can be stored in any different numeric type will vary from system to system. On my Windows machine, the maximum value for an integer is 2,147,483,647. You can find the actual maximum value for an integer on your system by using the following code in a Python Interactive Shell session:

```
import sys
print sys.maxint
2147483647 (My system)
```

Hexadecimal, octal, and binary numbers also fall under the Numeric data type umbrella.

Hexadecimal numbers are base 16. They range from 0 to 9 and A to F. Octal numbers are base 8 numbers. They range from 0 to 7. Binary numbers are base 2 numbers and only include 0 and 1. Examples of each follow:

Hexadecimal - 1B = 27 (decimal)
Octal - 033 = 27 (decimal)
Binary - 00011011 = 27 (decimal)

String

The string data type is a series of characters that is delimited by quotation marks (either single or double). Strings will be discussed seperately in Chapter 4. An example of strings would include:

```
'This is a string'
"3.14159"
```

Lists, Tuples, and Dictionaries will be discussed in Chapter 6, but for now here is a quick description.

List

Lists are a way to create multiple values that are referenced by a single variable name with a zero-based index, similar to arrays in other programming languages. Lists use square brackets ("[ ]") to define them. An example would be:

```
ColorList = ['Red','Orange','Yellow','Green','Blue','Purple']
```

ColorList[2] would be the value 'Yellow.'

Tuple

Tuples are a number of values seperated by commas. The data within a tuple may consist of numbers, strings, and even other objects:

```
t = 3,42,'The time has come for all good men'
```

Like lists, tuples are referenced by a zero-based index. t[1] would be the value "42".

Dictionary

A dictionary is like a mini database in memory. Each item in a dictionary has two parts: a key and a value. Each item is referenced (usually) by its key. A dictionary uses curly brackets to define them:

```
dict = {"Fname":"Jack","LName":"Sprat"}
```

In this example, there are two sets of data in the 'dict' dictionary. 'Fname' is the key for the value 'Jack' and 'LName' is the key for the value 'Sprat.'

Data Type Conversion

There are several built-in functions to perform conversion from one data type to another.

int(s,[base])

Returns an integer from the string s. If base is provided, specifies what base to use for the conversion. *If the string is not that of a value (binary, hex, octal, integer, long, etc.), you will receive an error.*

```
>>> int('1001',2)
9
>>> int('FA',16)
250
```

long(s,[base])

Returns a long integer from the string s. If base is provided, it specifies what base to use for the conversion. If the string is not a valid number, it will return an error.

```
>>> long(30219568420)
30219568420L
```

float(s)

Returns a floating point number from the string s. If the string is not a valid number, this will return an error.

```
>>> d = '3.14159'
>>> e = float(d)
>>> e
3.14159
```

complex(real [,imaginary])

Creates a complex number.

```
>>> complex(3.14159)
(3.14159+0j)
>>> complex(-123.45)
(-123.45+0j)
>>> complex(32,43)
(32+43j)
```

str(x)

Returns a string based on the numeric value x. If (x) is not a valid number, this function will return an error.

```
>>> str(3.14159)
'3.14159'
```

tuple(s)

Returns a tuple based on sequence s. The sequence should be something like a string or a list.

```
>>> tuple([3,5,7])
(3, 5, 7)
>>> tuple('abcd')
('a', 'b', 'c', 'd')
```

list(s)

Returns a list based on sequence s. The sequence should be something like a string or a tuple.

```
>>> list((1,2,3))
[1, 2, 3]
>>> list('abcd')
['a', 'b', 'c', 'd']
```

set(l)

Returns a set based on sequence l. Sequence l must be a list.

```
>>> set([7,3,11])
set([11, 3, 7])
```

dict(s) (s must be sequence of (key,value) tuples)

Returns a dictionary from a list of tuples.

```
>>> dict([('fname','fred'),('value',1)])
{'value': 1, 'fname': 'fred'}
```

frozenset(s)

Returns a frozenset created from set s.

```
>>> s = set([7,3,1])
>>> frozenset(s)
frozenset([1, 3, 7])
```

chr(x)

Returns a character created from integer x in the range of 0 to 255.

```
>>> chr(65)
'A'
```

unichr(x)

Returns a unicode character created from integer x in the range (on most machines) of 0 to 0x10000.

```
>>> unichr(1000)
u'\u03e8'
```

ord(c)

Returns the ascii value of character c.

```
>>> ord('M')
77
```

hex(x)

Returns a hexadecimal string created from integer x.

```
>>> hex(23)
'0x17'
```

oct(x)

Returns an octal string created from integer x.

```
>>> oct(32)
'040'
```

CHAPTER 3

▪ ▪ ▪

Operators

Python supports several operators. Here, we review some of the key ones.

Arithmetic Operators

We use the arithmetic operators to do simple math on two variables or literals. Be sure to only try to use arithmetic operators on like types. For example, if you try to add a string value to a integer (3 + " is a number") you will get an error.

+ Addition

Adds the left value to the right:

```
>>> lvariable = 5
>>> sum = lvariable + 3
>>> sum
8
```

– Subtraction

Subtracts the right value from left:

```
>>> lvariable = 5
>>> difference = lvariable - 3
>>> difference
2
```

* Multiplication

Multiplies left value by right:

```
>>> lvariable = 5
>>> product = lvariable * 3
>>> product
15
```

/ Division

Divides left value by right. Integer divided by integer returns an integer. Right-side value can not be zero:

```
>>> quotient = 5 / 3 # integer/integer
>>> quotient
1
>>> quotient = 5.2 / 3.1 # float/float
>>> quotient
1.6774193548387097
>>> quotient = 3.14159 / 7 # float/integer
>>> quotient
0.44879857142857144
>>> quotient = 7 / 3.14159 # integer/float
>>> quotient
2.2281710853421357
>>> quotient = 5 / 0
Traceback (most recent call last):
File "<stdin>", line 1, in <module>
ZeroDivisionError: integer division or modulo by zero
```

% Modulus

Divides left value by right and returns the remainder:

```
>>> remainder = 5 % 3
>>> remainder
2
>>> remainder = 3 % 5
>>> remainder
3
```

** Exponent

Left value raised to the power of the right:

```
>>> exp = 2 ** 3
>>> exp
8
>>> exp = 2.1 ** 3
>>> exp
9.261000000000001
```

// Floor Division

Division, but with the decimal values rounded down to the nearest integer:

```
>>> quotient = 5.2 // 3.1
>>> quotient
1.0
```

Comparison Operators

When we want to compare two values to each other, as in equality (a is equal to b), we use comparison operators. Unlike many other programming languages Python comparison operators may differ.

In the following examples, assume the following:

```
a = 5
b = 3
```

==

Checks to see if left variable is equal to right. Please note that when using floating point numbers (floats) that there will be times that the calculations do not act as you might expect due to the way floating point numbers are stored in Python. When you need precise calculations, use the decimal library:

```
>>> print(a == b)
False
>>> test = 1.1+2.2
>>> test == 3.3
False # test is actually 3.3000000000000003
```

== (Strings)

Comparison of strings, lists, and other objects is very similar to that of numbers:

```
Str1 = "This is a test"
Str2 = "This was a test"
Str1 == Str2
False
Lst1 = [1,2,3,4]
Lst2 = Lst1
Lst2 == Lst1
True
```

15

!=

Checks to see if left variable is NOT equal to right (3.x and 2.x):

```
Python 2.x
>>> print(a != b)
True
Python 3.x
>>> print(a != b)
True
```

<>

Checks to see if left variable is NOT equal to right (2.x only):

```
Python 2.x
>>> print(a <> b)
True
Python 3.x (use !=)
>>> print(a <> b)
File "<stdin>", line 1
print(a <> b)
^
SyntaxError: invalid syntax
```

>

Checks to see if left variable is greater than right:

```
>>> print(a > b)
True
```

<

Checks to see if left variable is less than right:

```
>>> print(a < b)
False
```

>=

Checks to see if left variable is greater than or equal to right:

```
>>> print(a >= b)
True
```

<=

Checks to see if left variable is less than or equal to right:

```
>>> print(a <= b)
False
```

Assignment Operators

Assignment operators, as we have seen earlier, assigns and/or modifies a value to a variable.

=

Assignment operator. Assigns the value on right to variable on left:

```
>>> a = 3
>>> a
3
```

+=

Add and assign or increment operator. Adds value on right to left variable:
```
>>> a = 3
>>> a += 3
>>> a
6
```

−=

Subtract and assign or decrement operator. Subtracts value on right from left variable:

```
>>> a = 3
>>> a -= 2
>>> a
1
```

*=

Multiply and assign. Multiplies right value to left value:

```
>>> a = 3
>>> a *= 2
>>> a
6
```

/=

Divide and assign. Divides right value from left value:

```
>>> a = 3
>>> a /= 2.0
>>> a
1.5
```

%=

Modulus and assign:

```
>>> a = 3
>>> a %= 2
>>> a
1
```

**=

Exponent and assign:

```
>>> a = 3
>>> a **= 2
>>> a
9
```

//=

Floor Division and assign:

```
>>> a = 5.0
>>> a //= 3.0
>>> a
1.0
```

Logical Operators

Python provides three operators for logical operations: and, or and not. These operators allow us to compare two values without having to rely on normal equality considerations. You could think of logical operators as sort of a high level binary evaluation.

and

Logical AND – if both values are True (or in many cases, nonzero), then returns a true value:

```
a = 0
b = 8
if (a and b):
    print 'true'
else:
    print 'false'
```

false

or

Logical OR – if either value is True, returns a true value:

```
a = 0
b = 8
if (a or b):
    print 'true'
else:
    print 'false'
```
true

not

Logical NOT – reverses the operator. True becomes False and False becomes True:

```
a = 0
b = 8
if not(a and b):
    print 'true'
else:
    print 'false'
```
true

Membership and Identity Operators

We use membership operators to test to see if a particular value is a member of (or is included in) a particular object like a list or dictionary. The identity operators check to see if the two objects are the same.

In

Returns True if x is in y:

```
>>> a = "This is the time"
>>> 'is' in a
True
>>> lst = [1,2,4,7,9]
>>> 2 in lst
True
>>> 8 in lst
False
```

not in

Returns True if x is NOT in y:

```
>>> a = "This is the time"
>>> 'frog' not in a
True
```

is

Returns True if variables on each side refers to the same object:

```
>>> c = list(['a','b','c'])
>>> d = c
>>> c is d
True
```

is not

Returns False if variables on each side refers to the same object:

```
>>> c = list(['a','b','c'])
>>> d = c
>>> c is not d
False
```

Bitwise Operators

These operators perform bit by bit operations on binary values.

Binary numbers consist of 1s and 0s called bits. In a 4-bit binary number, the value will range from 0 to 15. In an 8-bit number, the value will range from 0 to 255. Each bit position has a value starting from right to left. A 1 in any position gets counted to make a standard decimal number. For a 4-bit number, the positions are 1,2,4,8. It is easy to see that the value for each position is doubled.

```
0000 0
0001 1
0010 2
0011 3
0100 4
```

...

In the following examples, assume the following:

```
a = 00011000 (24)
b = 00001000 (8)
```

&

Binary AND
Compares bit by bit the two values; if the bits are both 1 in any given position, then the result is 1 for that bit position:

```
>>> a & b
8 (00001000)
00011000
00001000
Equals
00001000 (8)
```

|

Binary OR
Compares bit by bit the two values and if either of the bits are 1 in any given position, then the result is 1 for that bit position:

```
>>> a | b
24 (00011000)
00011000
00001000
Equals
00011000 (24)
```

∧

Binary XOR.

Compares bit by bit the two values and if either of the bits are 1 **but not both bits**, then the result is 1 for that bit position:

```
>>> a ^ b
16 (00010000)
00011000
00001000
Equals
00010000 (16)
```

~

Binary Ones complement.

Ones complement is defined as the value that is obtained by inverting all the bits in the number. This then behaves like a negative value of the original value in some arithmetic operations:

```
a = 24 (00011000)
>>> ~a
-25
(11100111)
```

<<

Binary Shift Left.

Shifts all bits to the left. Zeros are inserted at the right side:

```
>>> a << 2
96 (00011000 Shift Left 2 = 01100000 = 64 + 32 = 96)
```

>>

Binary Shift Right.

Shifts all bits to the right by x positions. Zeros are inserted at the left side:

```
>>> a >> 2
6 (00011000 Shift Right 2 = 00000110 = 2 + 4 = 6)
```

Precedence of Operators

Precedence of operators is the order that the various operators are processed in calculations.

For example: If the calculation is 3 + 5 * 4 + 6, the answer would be 29. Multiplication takes precedence over addition, so the formula breaks down to 20 + 9 (5 * 4) + (3 + 6).

The precedence of evaluation is always overridden by the use of parentheses:

```
(3 + 5) * (4 + 6) = 112
3+5*4+10 = 33 (3 + 20 (5*4) + 10)
```

The following list shows precedence of the operators from lowest to highest:

- Lambda (Discussed in Chapter 7)
- If - else (Discussed in Chapter 5)
- or
- and
- not x
- in, not in, is, is not
- |
- ^
- &
- << , >>
- + , −
- *, / , //, %
- +x, −x, ~x
- **
- X[index], x[index:index], x(arguments...), x.attribute
- (expressions...), [expressions...], {key:value...},'expressions...'
- ()

CHAPTER 4

Strings

String objects exist in practically every programming language. A string is simply a series of characters assigned to a variable. Python strings are immutable, which means that once created, they can not be changed. String assignments look like this:

```
s = 'Abcdefg'
```

Appending to Srings

Although Python strings are immutable, we can perform many operations on them, including appending other information to the string.

```
>>> a = "This is a test"
>>> a = a + " of strings"
>>> a
'This is a test of strings'
```

In this case, a copy of the string is made, the second string is appended to the copy, then the original is deleted and the new string is renamed to the old name.

String Functions

There are a number of built-in functions that are available for strings. Note that most of these functions also exist for other types of objects.

len()

Returns the length of the string.

```
>>> a = "The time has come"
>>> len(a)
17
```

min()

Returns the minimum (lowest ascii value) character within the string.

```
>>> a = "The time has come"
>>> min(a)
' '
```

max()

Returns the maximum (highest ascii value) character within the string.

```
>>> a = "The time has come"
>>> max(a)
't'
```

s1 in s2

Returns True if s1 is in string.

```
>>> a = "The time has come"
>>> "has" in a
True
>>> "not" in a
False
```

s1 not in s2

```
>>> a = "The time has come"
>>> "not" not in a
True
```

s1 + s2

Concatenates s2 to s1.

```
>>> a = "The time has come"
>>> b = " for all good men"
>>> c = a + b
>>> c
'The time has come for all good men'
```

s[x]

Returns the single character at position x within the string (zero based). Also known as the *slice* function. To get the slice starting at position x to the end of the string, use s[x:].

```
>>> c
'The time has come for all good men'
>>> c[7]
'e'
>>> c[7:]
'e has come for all good men'
```

s[x1:x2]

Returns a slice of the string starting at x1 and going to x2 (zero based). X2 should be considered starting point + length of string to be returned.

If we want to get 8 characters from the string "The time has come for all good men" starting with the word "time," we would use c[4:12], as 4 is the zero-based fourth character in the string and we want 8 characters, which is position 12. This can be confusing to beginning users.

```
>>> c
'The time has come for all good men'
>>> c[4:12] # Want 8 characters (4 + 8 = 12)
'time has'
```

s[x1:x2:x3]

Similar to s[x1:x2] but with an additional parameter of number of characters to step. You can also use a negative number as the step parameter. A -1 would reverse the string starting from the last character. A -2 would give every other character starting from the end.

```
>>> c
'The time has come for all good men'
>>> c[4:12:2]
'tm a'
>>> c[::-1]
'nem doog lla rof emoc sah emit ehT'
>>> c[::-2]
'nmdo l o mcshei h'
```

String Methods

Methods differ from functions in that methods pertain to a specific object. For example, the length of a string uses the len() function. To get the number of times that the letter 't' occurs in the variable str1, which is the string "This is the time," we would use str1.count('t').

str.capitalize()

Returns a string where the first character of the string is set to uppercase and the rest is lowercase.

```
>>> d = "this is a test"
>>> d.capitalize()
'This is a test'
```

str.center(width[,fillchar])

Returns a string where the original string is center justified filled with fillchar to the width of width. The default fill character is a space. If original string length is longer or equal width, the original string is returned. This is similar to ljust() and rjust().

```
>>> c = "A Test"
>>> c.center(10)
' A Test '
>>> c.center(10,"*")
'**A Test**'
```

str.count(sub[,start[,end]])

Returns the number of instances of sub. Optional start and end parameters limit the search within the string.

```
>>> s = "This is the time"
>>> s.count("t")
2
>>> s.count("T")
1
```

str.decode([encoding[,errors]])

Returns a decoded strinng using the encoding codec. Usually used for Unicode strings. Possible parameters for the errors parameter are 'ignore,' 'replace,' 'xmlcharrefreplace,' 'backslashreplace,' 'strict' and others registered in codecs.register_error(). Defaults to 'strict.'

Python 2.x:

```
>>> s = "This is the time"
>>> d = s.encode('UTF-8',errors='strict')
>>> d
'This is the time'
>>> d.decode('UTF-8',errors='strict')
u'This is the time' # the leading 'u' denotes unicode.
```

Python 3.x:

```
>>> s = "This is the time"
>>> d = s.encode('UTF-8',errors='strict')
>>> d
b'This is the time' # the leading 'b' denotes a byte array.
>>> d.decode('UTF-8',errors='strict')
'This is the time'
```

str.encode([encoding[,errors]])

Returns an encoded string using the encoding codec. Usually used for Unicode strings.

```
>>> d = s.encode('UTF-8',errors='strict')
>>> d
'This is the time'
```

str.endswith(suffix[,start[,end]])

Returns True if string ends with suffix. Optional start and end limits the search within the string. Suffix can be a tuple of suffixes to search for.

```
>>> s
'This is the time'
>>> s.endswith('time')
True
```

str.expandtabs([tabsize])

Returns a copy of the string with all tabs replaced by one or more space characters. Default tab size is 8. In the following example, the "\t" character equates to a tab character.

```
>>> t = "Item1\tItem2\tItem3\tItem4"
>>> t
'Item1\tItem2\tItem3\tItem4'
>>> t.expandtabs(6)
'Item1 Item2 Item3 Item4'
```

str.find(substring[,start[,end]])

Returns the index of the first instance of substring is located within the string. Returns -1 if sub is not found. Index is zero-based. The start and end parameters allow you to narrow the find.

```
>>> b = "This is the time of the party"
>>> b.find("the")
8
>>> b.find("the",11)
20
```

str.format(*args,**kwargs)

Returns a string that is formatted using a formatting operation. This is a variable substitution function. Replaces the % formatting operation. See the section on formatting later in this chapter. The *args and **kwargs parameters are there when an unknown set of arguments may be provided and/or a keyword/value set needs to be passed.

```
>>> a = 3.14159
>>> b = "PI = {0}".format(a)
>>> b
'PI = 3.14159'
```

str.format_map(mapping) Python 3.x only

Similar to str.format, but the mapping parameter is used directly and not copied to a dictionary. In the following example, there are two items that will be substituted in the string, one {vocation} and the other {location}. We have created a class called Helper, which expects a dictionary key/value pair. If the key/value pair is provided, then we get that value. If not, the __missing__ routine is called and the key is returned. Using the .format_map routine, each key in the format function definition is sent into the Helper class. Because we are only passing the dictionary information for {vocation}, when it gets to {location}, the Helper routine returns "location" which is used in the string.

```
>>> class Helper(dict):
...     def __missing__(self,key):
...         return key
>>> a = 'Fred is a {vocation} at
{location}'.format_map(Helper(vocation='teacher'))
>>> a
'Fred is a teacher at location'
```

str.index(substring[,start[,end]])

Works like find but raises ValueError error if substring is not found. Because this raises an error if the substring is not found, it is considered a better option for flow control than the .find() method.

str.isalnum()

Returns True if all characters in string are alphanumeric.

```
>>> f = "This is the time" # includes white space, so false
>>> f.isalnum()
False
>>> e = "abcdef1234"
>>> e.isalnum()
True
```

str.isalpha()

Returns True if all characters in string are alphabetic.

```
>>> e = "abcdef1234" # includes numerics, so false
>>> e.isalpha()
False
>>> g = "abcdef"
>>> g.isalpha()
True
```

str.isdecimal() Python 3.x only

Returns True if all characters in the string are decimal characters. Works on Unicode representations of decimal numbers.

```
e = 12.34
e.isdecimal()
False
e = "\u00B2"
e.isdecimal()
True
```

str.isdigit()

Returns True if all characters in string are digits.

```
>>> a
3.14159
>>> str(a).isdigit() # contains a decimal point, so false
False
>>> b = "12345"
>>> b.isdigit()
True
```

str.isidentifier() Python 3.x only

Returns True if the string is a valid identifier. Valid identifiers like the way we name variables. An example of an invalid identifier would be a string that starts with a "%."

```
>>> a = "print"
>>> a.isidentifier()
True
>>> a = "$"
>>> a.isidentifier()
False
```

str.islower()

Returns True if all characters in string are lowercase.

```
>>> a = 'the time has come for'
>>> a.islower()
True
```

str.isprintable() Python 3.x only

Returns True if all characters in string are printable or if the string is empty.

str.isspace()

Returns True if all characters in string are only whitespace.

str.istitle()

Returns True if the entire string is a titlecased string (only first character of each word is uppercase).

```
>>> a = 'The Time Has Come'
>>> a.istitle()
True
>>> b = 'The TIme Has Come'
>>> b.istitle()
False
```

str.isupper()

Returns True if entire string is uppercased string.

```
>>> c = "ABCDEFGH"
>>> c.isupper()
True
>>> b
'The TIme Has Come'
>>> b[4].isupper() # Is the 5th character in 'b' uppercased?
True
```

str.join(iterable)

Returns a string that has each value in iterable concatinated into the string using a separator. Many times, it might just be easier to concatenate the strings with the "+" sign.

```
>>> a = ","
>>> a.join(["a","b","c"])
'a,b,c'
```

str.ljust(width[,fillchar])

Returns a string where the original string is left justified padded with fillchar to the width of width. If original string length is longer or equal width, the original string is returned. Similar to center(), rjust().

```
>>> a = "The time"
>>> a.ljust(15,"*")
'The time*******'
```

str.lower()

Returns a copy of string with all characters converted to lowercase.

```
>>> a
'The time'
>>> a.lower()
'the time'
```

str.lstrip([chars])

Returns a copy of string with leading [chars] removed. If [chars] is omitted, any leading whitespace characters will be removed.

```
>>> a = " This is a test"
>>> a.lstrip()
'This is a test'
>>> a.lstrip(" This")
'a test'
```

str.maketrans(x[,y]]) Python 3.x only

Returns a translation table for the translate method. This table can be used by the translate method (see later in this chapter). In the case of the example here, any of the characters in the inalpha string will be changed, or translated, to the corresponding character in the outalpha string. So a=1, b=2, c=3, and so on.

```
>>> inalpha = "abcde"
>>> outalpha = "12345"
>>> tex = "This is the time for all good men"
>>> trantab = str.maketrans(inalpha,outalpha)
>>> print(tex.translate(trantab))
This is th5 tim5 for 1ll goo4 m5n
```

str.partition(sep)

Returns a 3-tuple that contains the part before the separator, the separator itself and the part after the separator. If the separator is not found, the 3-tuple contains the string, followed by two empty strings.

```
>>> b = "This is a song.mp3"
>>> b.partition(".")
('This is a song', '.', 'mp3')
```

str.replace(old,new[,count])

Returns a copy of the string with all occurences of old replaced by new. If the optional count is provided, only the first count occurances are replaced. Notice in the sample that the "is" in "This" is also replaced becoming "Thwas."

```
>>> b = "This is a song.mp3"
>>> b.replace('is','was')
'Thwas was a song.mp3'
```

str.rfind(sub[,start[,end]])

Returns the index of the last instance of sub-substring within string. Returns -1 if sub is not found. Index is zero-based.

```
>>> b = "This is the time of the party"
>>> b.rfind("the")
20
```

str.rindex(sub[,start[,end]])

Works like rfind but raises ValueError error if substring sub is not found.

str.rjust(width[,fillchar])

Returns a string where the original string is right-justified padded with fillchar to the width of width. If original string length is longer or equal width, the original string is returned. Similar to center(), ljust().

```
>>> a = "The time"
>>> a.rjust(15,"*")
'*******The time'
```

str.rpartition(sep)

Like partition(), but returns the part of the string before the last occurrence of sep as the first part of the 3-tuple.

```
>>> b = 'This is a song.mp3'
>>> b.rpartition(' ')
('This is a', ' ', 'song.mp3')
```

str.rsplit([sep[,maxsplit]])

Returns a list of tokens in the string using sep as a delimiter string. If maxsplit is provided, the list will be the RIGHTMOST set. Similar to split().

```
>>> a = "This is the time"
>>> a.rsplit(" ",2)
['This is', 'the', 'time']
```

str.rstrip([chars])

Returns a copy of the string with trailing characters [chars] removed. If [chars] is empty or not provided, whitespace is removed.

```
>>> a = " This is a test "
>>> a.rstrip()
'This is a test'
```

str.split([sep[,maxsplit]])

Returns a list of words in the string using sep as a delimiter string. If maxsplit is provided, the list will be the LEFTMOST set. Similar to rsplit().

```
>>> a = "This is the time"
>>> a.split()
['This', 'is', 'the', 'time']
```

str.splitlines([keepends])

Returns a list of the lines in the string, breaking the string at line boundries. Linebreaks are NOT included in the resulting list unless the [keepends] is given and True.

```
>>> t = "The time has come\r\nFor all good men"
>>> t.splitlines()
['The time has come', 'For all good men']
>>> t.splitlines(True)
['The time has come\r\n', 'For all good men']
```

str.startswith(prefix[,start[,end]])

Returns True if string starts with the prefix otherwise returns false. Using optional start,end parameters will limit the search within that portion of the string. Similar to endswith().

```
>>> a = "This is a test"
>>> a.startswith('This')
True
>>> a.startswith('This',4)
False
```

str.strip([chars])

Returns a copy of the string where all leading and trailing characters are removed. If argument is blank, removes all whitespace characters. If argument is provided, all values in the argument are removed.

```
>>> c = "thedesignatedgeek.net"
>>> c.strip('thenet')
'designatedgeek.'
```

str.swapcase()

Returns a copy of the string where the uppercase characters are converted to lowercase and the lowercase converted to uppercase.

```
>>> a = "The Time Has Come"
>>> a.swapcase()
'tHE tIME hAS cOME'
```

str.title()

Returns a copy of the string where the first character of each word is uppercased. Words with apostrophes may cause unexpected results.

```
>>> a = "Fred said they're mine."
>>> a.title()
"Fred Said They'Re Mine."
```

str.translate(table[,deletechars]) Python 2.x

Returns a string that have all characters in the translate table replaced. Use the maketrans method from the string library to create the translation table. The optional deletechars parameter will remove any characters in the parameter string from the return string. To just delete certain characters, pass None for the table parameter.

```
>>> from string import maketrans # Import the maketrans function from the
string library.
>>> intable = 'aeiou'
>>> outtable = '12345'
>>> trantable = maketrans(intable,outtable)
>>> a = "The time has come"
>>> a.translate(trantable)
'Th2 t3m2 h1s c4m2'
>>> a.translate(None,'aeiou')
'Th tm hs cm'
```

str.translate(table) Python 3.x

Very similar to the Python 2.x version of .translate() with the following exceptions.

> There is no deletechars optional parameter.

> Maketrans is a method that does not need to be imported from the string library.

str.upper()

Returns a copy of the string with all characters converted to uppercase.

```
>>> a = "The time has come"
>>> a.upper()
'THE TIME HAS COME'
```

str.zfill(width)

Returns a copy of a numeric string that is left filled with zeros to the string length of width (length). If the length of the string is less than or equal to width, the original string is returned.

```
>>> b = "3.1415"
>>> b.zfill(10)
'00003.1415'
>>> b.zfill(5) # the width of b (length) is 6
'3.1415'
```

Print Statement

Python 2.x allows you to use the following format when using the print statement:

```
>>> print 'The time has come for all good men'
The time has come for all good men
```

However, Python 3.x will not accept this format. The Python 3.x format requires parentheses around the string to print.

```
>>> print('The time has come for all good men')
The time has come for all good men
```

For ease of transition between the two versions, Python 2.7 has backported the Python 3.x print format.

Python 2.x String Formatting

Formatting in Python 2.x uses a 'string % value' type field replacement formatting option. This allows much more control over the final output than simply trying to concatinate different strings and variables for the print or other output functions.

```
>>> print '%s uses this type of formatting system' % "Python 2.7"
Python 2.7 uses this type of formatting system
```

The '%s' indicates that a string should be place at that position and the '%' at the end of the line provides the value that should be substituted. This could be a literal (as in the case above) or a variable.

To provide an integer value, use the '%d' field. You can also provide certain formatting options along with the field designator. In the case here, the '%03d' means to format an integer to have a width of 3 and to zero fill on the left.

```
>>> print '%03d goodies in this bag' % 8
008 goodies in this bag
```

To provide more than one value to the substitution group, enclose the values in parenthese.

```
>>> print '%d - %f Numbers' % (3,3.14159)
3 - 3.141590 Numbers
```

You can also use named variables in the output. In the following example, the '%(frog)s' uses the value 'Python' from the key 'frog' in the provided dictionary.

```
>>> print '%(frog)s can print nicely %(num)d ways' %
{'frog':'Python','num':2}
Python can print nicely 2 ways
```

Table 4-1 lists the various flags that can be used to modify the way the substitution will work.

***Table 4-1.** Substitution Flags for the print statement*

Flag	Meaning
#	The value conversion will use the alternate form (hex, octal, binary, etc). See Table 4-2.
0	The conversion will be zero-padded for numeric values.
–	The conversion value is left adjusted (overrides the "0" conversion).
	Space—A blank should be left before a positive number.
+	A sign character (+ or –) will preceed the conversion (overrides the space conversion).

Table 4-2 shows the possible formatting of substitution keys.

Table 4-2. *Substitution keys for the print statement*

Conversion	Meaning
'd'	Signed integer decimal
'i'	Signed integer decimal
'u'	Obsolete—identical to 'd'
'o'	Signed octal value
'x'	Signed hexadecimal—lowercase
'X'	Signed hexadecimal—uppercase
'f'	Floating point decimal
'e'	Floting point exponential—lowercase
'E'	Floating point exponential—uppercase
'g'	Floating point format—uses lowercase exponential format if exponent is less than -4 or not less than precision, decimal format otherwise
'G'	Floating point format—uses uppercase exponential format if exponent is less than -4 or not less than precision, decimal format otherwise
'c'	Single character
'r'	String (converts valid Python object using repr())
's'	String (converts valid Python object using str())
'%'	No argument is converted, results in a '%' character

Python 3.x String Formatting

Python 3.x uses a different formatting system, which is more powerful than the system that Python 2.x uses. The print statement is now a function. Format strings use the curly brackets "{}" to create the replacement fields. Anything that is not contained within the brackets will be considered a literal and no converstion will be done on it. If you have the need to include curly brackets as a literal, you can escape it by using '{{' and '}}.' This formatting system has been backported to Python 2.6 and Python 2.7.

The basic format string is like this:

```
print('This is a value - {0}, as is this - {1}'.format(3,4))
```

Where the numbers 0 and 1 refer to the index in the value list, and will print out as follows:

This is a value - 3, as is this - 4

It is not necessary to include the numbers inside the brackets. The values presented in the parameter list will be substituded in order.

```
>>> print('Test {} of {}'.format(1,2))
Test 1 of 2
```

You can also use keys into a dictionary as the reference within the brackets, like in Python 2.x.

Example of zero padded format for floating point values. {:[zero pad][width]. [precision]}

```
>>> a = "This is pi - {:06.2f}".format(3.14159)
>>> a
'This is pi - 003.14'
```

You can align text and specify width by using the following alignment flags:
:<x Left Align with a width of x
:>x Right Align with a width of x
:^x Center Align with a width of x

```
>>> a = '{:<20}'.format('left')
>>> a
'left                '
>>> a = '{:>20}'.format('right')
>>> a
'               right'
>>> a = '{:^20}'.format('center')
>>> a
'       center       '
```

You can also specify the fill character.

```
>>> a = '{:*>10}'.format(3.14)
>>> a
'******3.14'
```

Example of date and time formatting.

```
>>> import datetime
>>> d = datetime.datetime(2013,9,4,9,54,15)
>>> print('{:%m/%d/%y %H:%M:%S}'.format(d))
09/04/13 09:54:15
```

Thousands separator.

```
>>> a = 'big number {:,}'.format(72819183)
>>> a
'big number 72,819,183'
```

Table 4-3. *Format Specifiers using examples*

Specifier	Description
:<20	Left Align to a width of 20.
:>20	Right Align to a width of 20.
:^20	Center Align to a width of 20.
:06.2f	Zero pad with precision for floating point number.
:*>10	Asterisk pad right align to a width of 10.
:=10	Padding is placed after the sign, if any but before digits. ONLY works for numeric types.
:+20	Force a sign before the number left padded to a width of 20.
:-20	Force a sign before negative numbers only, left padded to a width of 20.
: 20	Force a leading space on positive numbers or "-" on negative numbers, left padded to a width of 20.
:,	Force thousands comma for numeric.
:.2%	Expresses percentage (.975 results in 97.50%)
:%M/%d/%Y	Type specific usage. In this case datetime.
0:#x	Formats an integer as a hex value 0xhh.
0:#o	Formats an integer as an octal value 0oxx.
0:#b	Formats an integer as a binary value 0bxxxxxx.

## CHAPTER 5

Conditional Statements

Conditional statements are an important part of many programs. They allow logic control of our programs. There are three main conditional statement types in Python. If / Elif / Else conditionals, For loops and While loops.

IF / ELIF / ELSE Statements

The if statements allow us to check the truth of a statement or statements and apply logic to the various possibilities. The if statement is simple at its heart.

```
if (statement) :
    # do the following code
    # do this line as well
# This line is NOT part of the if statement.
```

The statement starts with the 'if' keyword (the 'if' must be in lowercase) followed by the conditional expression then a colon character. The line(s) of code that you want to have executed if the statement is true, must be indented.
Assume that the variable a = 3 and the variable b = 7.

```
if a < b:
    print("a less than b")
```

a less than b

You can also add a second option so that if the first statement is not true, the program would run the alternate code. This is the else option. The 'else' phrase does not allow for any additional logic and must be followed by a colon.

```
if b < a:
    print("b less than a")
else:
    print("a less than b")
```

a less than b

If you have more than two options, you can use the elif option of the if / else statement. You can have as many elif statements as you need. The elif option must have some sort of logic and be followed by a colon.

```
if a == 3:
    print('a=3')
elif a == 4:
    print('a=4')
else:
    print('a not 3 or 4')

a=4
```

The if / elif / else statements must be at the main indention level with the logic indented.

```
a = 3
b = 4
c = 6
if a<b:
    d = 5
if (c<b) or (b<a):
    d = 2
    e = 5
elif (c<a):
    c = a
    a = 7
print a,b,c,d,e
7 4 6 5 5
```

For

The for keyword creates a loop controlled by the parameters that follow the assignment and will run a given number of times. Like the if statement, the keyword is followed by a sequence that will be "stepped" through (iteration), followed by a colon. All logic that is to be done within the loop is indented. In its simplest form, the for loop looks like this:

```
for x in range(3):
    print(x)

0
1
2
```

The range function will create a list based on the numbers that are in the parameter. In the earlier case, the list would be [0,1,2]. Under Python 2.x, you can use the xrange function instead of range. Xrange creates a generator that, in turn, creates the numbers as needed instead of creating a list, using less memory and makes the loop faster, because the numbers are generated as needed. If you are using Python 3.x, the xrange function is removed but is actually renamed as range.

```
for x in xrange(3):
    print(x)
```

```
0
1
2
```

As I stated earlier, the range function will create a list of values based on the parameter values. Because of this, you can use a list directly in your for statement.

```
for x in [1,2,3,4,5,6,7,8,9,10]:
    print x
```

```
1
2
3
4
5
6
7
8
9
10
```

You can also walk, or iterate, through a string as the list of values.

```
for char in "The time has come":
    print char
```
```
T
h
e

t
i
m
e

h
a
s
```

c
o
m
e

If you are iterating through a dictionary, you can the .iteritems() method of the dictionary object.

```
d = {'Key1':1,'Key2':2,'Key3':3}
for key,value in d.iteritems():
    print key,value
```

Key3 3
Key2 2
Key1 1

Another helpful option is to use the enumerate() function. This will allow you to iterate through a list and the count as well as the list value will be returned as a tuple.

```
mounts = ['Evans','Grays Peak','Longs Peak','Quandary']
for m in enumerate(mounts):
    print m
```

(0, 'Evans')
(1, 'Grays Peak')
(2, 'Longs Peak')
(3, 'Quandary')

Break

The break statement allows early termination of a loop (for or while). In this snippet, the for loop should run from 0 to 4, but when the loop hits the value of 3, the loop is terminated.

```
for x in range(5):
    if x == 3:
        break
    else:
        print(x)
```

0
1
2

Continue

The continue optional statement in a for loop allows for normal loop operation, but at the specified condition, the rest of the logic will be skipped for that iteration. In the snippet here, when the value in the for loop reaches 3, the print(x) logic will be skipped and the loop continues.

```
for x in range(5):
    if x == 3:
        continue
    else:
        print(x)
```

```
0
1
2
4
```

Else

The for loop also supports an optional else statement. Unlike the else statement used with the if conditional, it is more like the else in a try statement in that it always runs at the end of the loop.

```
for x in range(5):
    print x
else:
    print "The else"
```

```
0
1
2
3
4
The else
```

Pass

The pass statement will do nothing, which seems like a silly thing to have. However, it is actually valuable where you need to have a statement (like an option within an if clause) or to "stub" out a routine to be filled in later.

```
a = 3
if a == 2:
    pass
```

```
else:
    print("A != 2")
```

A != 2

```
def testfunction():
    pass
```

While

The while loop is used when you need your logic repeated until a certain condition is met, usually because you don't know how many times it will take. This could be because you are waiting for some condition to be met, like a timer expiring or a certain key press.

```
cntr = 0
while cntr < 11:
    print cntr
    cntr += 1
```
0
1
2
3
4
5
6
7
8
9
10

You can create an infinate loop as well, so you might want to be careful and create a way for the loop to break. If you end up in an infinate loop, you can press Ctrl + C to end the execution of your code.

```
cntr = 1
while cntr == 1:
    #do something forever.
```

## CHAPTER 6

Data Structures

Data structures are important for most any serious (and some not so serious) programs. They allow us to store groups of related data under a single variable name and access them quickly and logically. There are many types of data structures available under Python and each will be explained in the following sections.

Data Structure Example

Let's say that we need to keep a list of color names that are available to the end user and that list has the following values:

```
Red, Orange, Yellow, Green, Blue, Purple
```

We could simply create a number of distinct and separate variables to hold each value. On the other hand, we could use a list data structure to keep track of them under a single variable.

```
ColorList = ['Red','Orange','Yellow','Green','Blue','Purple']
```

By doing it this way, we can easliy access whichever color name we want by simply using an index into the ColorList variable.

```
print ColorList[2]
```

Will return "Yellow". Remember that the indexes are zero-based.

Digging Deeper

If we need to keep data, such as registration information, for the program that we are creating, we would need information like:

```
First Name, Last Name, Address, City, State, Postal Code
```

The first thought that springs to mind is to use a database to store this information. However, a quicker way to do it would be to use a dictionary structure. A dictionary (as you will see below), allows us to store data associated with a "key". By using the dictionary, we don't have the overhead of dealing with databases. We'll examine this later on when we discuss dictionaries later on in this chapter.

Lists

In other languages, there is a data structure called an Array. Going back to the shoe box analogy that I used back in Chapter 2, an array is simply a bunch of shoe boxes "glued" together that holds like data together under a single variable name. Python does not provide a native Array type. Instead, we have the List object.

A list is simply a collection of items that are accessible by an index number, similar to arrays. Unlike Arrays, Lists can contain any value like strings, integers, floating point numbers or other objects like dictionaries or even other lists. You can also mix types of data within a list. Lists are dynamic, so may be modified at any time.

To create a list by hand, you would use the square bracket characters "[" and "]". Each item in a list is separated by a comma.

```
MyList = ['This','is','a','list']
NumberList = [0,1,2,3,4,5,6]
MyEmptyList = []
SillyList = [3,'A String',42,'42',5,'The End']
```

To access a single item within a list, you would do it by accessing a list by its index value. Lists have zero-based indexes, so the first item in a list is index 0, the second item is index 1, and so on. Using the above example MyList:

```
>>> print MyList[2]
a
>>> print MyList[3]
list
>>> print MyList[0]
This
```

If you attempt to access the index of a list that does not exist (index position 4 in the MyList list for example), you will get an error.

To walk (or iterate) through the entire list from beginning to end, you can use a simple for loop:

```
for i in range(0,len(MyList)):
    print MyList[i]

This
is
a
list
```

An alternative way to do this is to something like the following code, which some programmers find simpler and more "pythonic" and at the same time produces the same output:

```
for elem in MyList:
    print elem
```

You can also convert other types of data structures to a list. In the example below, the variable t is a tuple.

```
>>> t = (1,2,3)
>>> l = list(t)
>>> l
[1, 2, 3]
```

List Functions

The following built-in operators are available to the List object.

len(L)

Returns the number of items in a list.

```
>>> l = [1,2,3,4,5,6,7]
>>> len(l)
7
```

min(L)

Returns the minimum value in a list.

```
>>> l = [1,2,3,4,5,6,7]
>>> min(l)
1
```

max(L) function

Returns the maximum value in a list.

```
>>> l = [1,2,3,4,5,6,7]
>>> max(l)
7
```

x in L

Returns True if x is in the list L.

```
>>> l = [1,2,3,4,5,6,7]
>>> 42 in l
False
>>> 3 in l
True
```

x not in L

Returns True if x is NOT in the list L.

```
>>> l = [1,2,3,4,5,6,7]
>>> 42 not in l
True
```

L1 + L2

Concatenate L2 to the end of L1.

```
>>> l = [1,2,3,4,5,6,7]
>>> l2 = [9,10,11,12]
>>> l+l2
[1, 2, 3, 4, 5, 6, 7, 9, 10, 11, 12]
```

L[x]

Retrieve item in list at index position x (zero-based). This is pretty much the same thing as using an array in another language. If you need to have something that acts like a multidimensional array, which is not available in Python, you can use a list of lists.

```
>>> l = [1,2,3,4,5,6,7]
>>>l[3]
4
```

L[x1:x2]

Slice of list L from index position x1 to x2 (zero-based).

```
>>> l = [1,2,3,4,5,6,7]
>>> l[2:4]
[3, 4]
```

del(L[x])

Removes the item from list L at index position x (zero-based).

```
>>> l = ['F', 'E', 'D', 'C', 'B', 'A']
>>> del(l[2])
>>> l
['F', 'E', 'C', 'B', 'A']
```

List Methods

The following methods are available to lists.

.append(x)

Append the value in x to a list.

```
>>> l = [0,1,2,3,4]
>>> l.append(5)
>>> l
[0, 1, 2, 3, 4, 5]
```

.extend(L)

Append a list to another list. In the following example, l is modified, l2 is not.

```
>>> l = [0,1,2,3,4]
>>> l2 = [5,6,7]
>>> l.extend(l2)
>>> l
[0, 1, 2, 3, 4, 5, 6, 7]
```

.insert(i,x)

Insert a value x into list at index I. The following example inserts the value 5 at position 2 in the list.

```
>>> l = [0,1,2,3,4]
>>> l.insert(2,5)
>>> l
[0, 1, 5, 2, 3, 4]
```

If carefully used, lists with the .insert() and .pop() methods can be a quick and easy way to implement a LIFO (Last in, First Out) queue or stack.

.remove(x)

Removes the first item in the list that matches 'x'. An error occurs if the item does not exist. The following example removes the value 2 from the list. The second example tries to do it again but gets an error.

```
>>> l = [0,1,2,3,4,5]
>>> l.remove(2)
>>> l
[0, 1, 3, 4, 5]
>>> l.remove(2)
Traceback (most recent call last):
File "<stdin>", line 1, in <module>
ValueError: list.remove(x): x not in list
```

.pop([i])

Returns and removes the last item in the list if the optional index number is not included. If it is, it removes the item at that index (zero-based). The following example uses pop() to remove the last item in the list, then removes the item at index position 2.

```
>>> l = [0,1,2,3,4,5]
>>> l.pop()
5
>>> l.pop()
4
>>> l.pop(2)
2
>>> l
[0, 1, 3]
```

If carefully used, lists with the .insert() and .pop() methods can be a quick and easy way to implement a LIFO (Last in, First Out) queue or stack.

.index(x)

Returns the position of the item in the list.

The following example first shows the index position of the value 3 in the example list (which is 3). The second example shows the index position of the item "Oranges" in the list.

```
>>> l = [0,1,2,3,4,5]
>>> l.index(3)
3
>>> l1 = ['Apples','Oranges','Kiwi','Peach']
>>> l1
```

```
['Apples', 'Oranges', 'Kiwi', 'Peach']
>>> l1.index('Oranges')
1
```

.count(x)

Returns the count of the matching items in the list. If item is not in the list, it returns 0.

```
>>> l = [3,1,3,4,3,6,7,8]
>>> l.count(3)
3
>>> l.count(2)
0
```

.sort()

Sorts the list from low to high.

```
>>> l2 = [0,1,2,3,2,5,7,3,1,2,5]
>>> l2.sort()
>>> l2
[0, 1, 1, 2, 2, 2, 3, 3, 5, 5, 7]
```

.reverse()

Reverses the list.

```
>>> l = [0,1,2,3,4,5,6,7,8]
>>> l.reverse()
>>> l
[8, 7, 6, 5, 4, 3, 2, 1, 0]
>>> l = ['A','B','C','D','E','F']
>>> l.reverse()
>>> l
['F', 'E', 'D', 'C', 'B', 'A']
```

Dictionaries

Dictionaries are a very valuable tool in our Python arsenal. A dictionary is like a list, but it allows you to store data with a keyword attached as a matched pair with the data. Earlier in this book, I talked about the need for registration information in an imaginary program. The information that is needed would be:

```
First Name, Last Name, Address, City, State, Postal Code
```

A dictionary allows us to keep that information very easily. For each piece of data we have a key that is associated with it. The structure of the key/value pair is:

```
{Key:Value}
```

Each key within a dictionary must be unique, but the value may be repeated if needed. Curly brackets are used to set up the dictionary. Keys may be strings or numbers.

```
dict = {"Fname":"Jack","LName":"Sprat"}
```

You can create a blank dictionary by simply assiging a variable to an empty set of curly brackets.

```
Names = {}
```

You can add new key/value pairs to a dictionary.

```
>>> names = {'fname':'Fred','lname':'Frackel','city':'Aurora','state':'C
O'}>>> names['phone'] = '222-222-2222'
>>> names
{'lname': 'Frackel', 'city': 'Aurora', 'state': 'CO', 'fname': 'Fred',
'phone':'222-222-2222'}
```

To iterate (walk through) a dictionary you can use the .iteritems() built in function. Notice that dictionaries do not store the key/value pairs in any predefined order, so items might not appear in the order that it is entered:

```
>>> names = {'fname':'Fred','lname':'Frackel','city':'Aurora','state':'CO'}
>>> for key,value in names.iteritems():
...     print key,value
...
lname Frackel
city Aurora
state CO
fname Fred
>>>
```

Dictionary Functions

Dictionaries have the following built-in functions.

len(dictionary)

Returns the number of items in a dictionary.

```
>>> d = {'lname':'Frackel','fname':'Fred','city':'Aurora','state':'CO'}
>>> len(d)
4
```

dict(list)

Creates a dictionary from a list provided and the list must contain at least one two-element tuple. The first element in the tuple is the key and the second is the value.

```
>>> d2 = dict([('one',1),('two',2),('three',3)])
>>> d2
{'three': 3, 'two': 2, 'one': 1}
```

Dictionary Methods

Dictionaries have the following built-in methods:

.clear()

Removes all items from a dictionary.

```
>>> test = {'one':'1','two':'2','three':'3'}
>>> test
{'three': '3', 'two': '2', 'one': '1'}
>>> test.clear()
>>> test
{}
```

.copy()

To make a copy of a dictionary, use the .copy() method. This is a shallow copy, which means that the content of the dictionary is not copied directly by value, but by reference and points to the actual original dictionary.

```
>>> first = {'a':1,'b':2,'c':3}
>>> clone = first.copy()
>>> first
{'a': 1, 'b': 2, 'c': 3}
>>> clone
{'a': 1, 'b': 2, 'c': 3}
```

.get(key[,default])

Returns a single value by key from a dictionary. Unlike the .pop() method, this does not remove the key/value pair from the dictionary. If key does not exist in dictionary, value from the optional default parameter is returned. If default is not given, returns None.

```
>>> names = {'lname': 'Frackel', 'city': 'Aurora', 'state': 'CO', 'fname':
'Fred', 'phone':'222-222-2222'}
>>> names
{'lname': 'Frackel', 'city': 'Aurora', 'state': 'CO', 'fname': 'Fred',
'phone':'222-222-2222'}
>>> names.get('lname')
'Frackel'
```

.has_key(key)

Returns True if the key exists in the dictionary. This method has been depreceated and the suggested way to check is to use key in d.

```
>>> names = {'lname': 'Frackel', 'city': 'Aurora', 'state': 'CO', 'fname':
'Fred', 'phone':'222-222-2222'}
>>> names.has_key('city')
True
>>> names.has_key('address')
False
```

.items( )

Returns a list of all key/value pairs in a dictionary. Notice that this is a nonsorted list and is not in the order that the data was entered.

```
>>> names = {'lname': 'Frackel', 'city': 'Aurora', 'state': 'CO', 'fname':
'Fred', 'phone':'222-222-2222'}
>>> names.items()
[('lname', 'Frackel'), ('city', 'Aurora'), ('state', 'CO'), ('fname',
'Fred'), ('phone', '222-222-2222')]
```

.keys( )

To get a list of keys from a dictionary, use the built in function .keys(). Notice that this is a nonsorted list and is not in the order that the keys were entered.

```
>>> names = {'lname': 'Frackel', 'city': 'Aurora', 'state': 'CO', 'fname':
'Fred'}
>>> names.keys()
['lname', 'city', 'state', 'fname']
```

To get a list of keys from a dictionary that is sorted, assign the return values from the .keys() function to a list then apply the .sort() function to that variable.

```
>>> names={'lname': 'Frackel', 'city': 'Aurora', 'state': 'CO', 'fname':
'Fred'}
>>> namekeys = names.keys()
>>> namekeys.sort()
>>> namekeys
['city', 'fname', 'lname', 'state']
```

.pop(key[,default])

Removes and returns the value of an item in the dictionary based on the key provided. If default is not given and the key does not exist, a KeyError is raised.

```
>>> names = {'lname': 'Frackel', 'city': 'Aurora', 'state': 'CO', 'fname':
'Fred','address':'123 Main Street'}
>>> names.pop('address')
'123 Main Street'
>>> names
{'lname': 'Frackel', 'city': 'Aurora', 'state': 'CO', 'fname': 'Fred',
'phone':'222-222-2222'}
```

.setdefault(key[,default])

Returns a value from the supplied key, if it exists. If not, it enters the key as a new item with the supplied default value.

```
>>> d1
{'a': 1, 'c': 3, 'b': 2, 'e': 0, 'd': 4}
>>> d1.setdefault('c',6)
3
>>> d1.setdefault('f',6)
6
>>> d1
{'a': 1, 'c': 3, 'b': 2, 'e': 0, 'd': 4, 'f': 6}
```

.update(other)

Updates the dictionary with the key/value pair provided in other. This will overwrite existing keys. Returns None. The other parameter can be either a tuple or list providing the key/value pair(s), or another dictionary.

```
>>> names = {'lname': 'Frackel', 'city': 'Aurora', 'state': 'CO', 'fname': 'Fred'}
>>> names.update({'address':'123 Main Street'})
>>> names
    {'lname': 'Frackel', 'city': 'Aurora', 'state': 'CO', 'fname': 'Fred',
'phone':'222-222-2222', 'address': '123 Main Street'}
```

.values( )

Returns a list of all values in a dictionary. The list returned is unsorted and may not be in the order that the data was entered. Using the list after the above update:

```
>>> names
{'lname': 'Frackel', 'city': 'Aurora', 'state': 'CO', 'fname': 'Fred',
'phone':'222-222-2222'}
>>> names.values()

['Frackel', 'Aurora', 'CO', 'Fred', '222-222-2222']
```

Tuples

A tuple is another kind of sequence data type. Tuples are a number of values seperated by commas. The data within a tuple may consist of numbers, strings and even other objects.

```
>>> t = 3,42,'The time has come for all good men'
>>> t
(3, 42, 'The time has come for all good men')
>>> t[0]
3
>>> t[2]
'The time has come for all good men'
```

Tuples are immutable objects, which mean that once it has been created, it can not be changed.

```
>>> t[0] = 73
Traceback (most recent call last):
 File "<stdin>", line 1, in <module>
TypeError: 'tuple' object does not support item assignment
```

Although a tuple is immutable, it can contain mutable objects like lists.

```
>>> t1 = [1,2,3],['a','b','c']
>>> t1
([1, 2, 3], ['a', 'b', 'c'])
>>> t1[0]
[1, 2, 3]
>>> t1[0][1] = 4
>>> t1
([1, 4, 3], ['a', 'b', 'c'])
```

You can also assign the values within a tuple to mutable variables.

```
>>> x,y = t1
>>> x
[1, 4, 3]
>>> y
['a', 'b', 'c']
```

Sets

Sets are an unordered collection with no duplicate elements. Sets are mutable (may be changed).

In the snippet below, you will see that we use the string 'This is a test' as the data for the set. When we get the actual data used in the set, there are only eight values. All other values are discarded because they are duplicates. Notice also that when the set is displayed, it is actually a list.

```
>>> settest = set('This is a test')
>>> settest
set(['a', ' ', 'e', 'i', 'h', 's', 'T', 't'])

>>> 'a' in settest
True
>>> 'b' in settest
False
```

Set Functions

The following functions are available for sets.

len(set)

Returns the length or count if items within the set.

```
>>> c
set([2, 3, 4, 5, 6, 7, 8, 9, 11])
>>> len(c)
9
```

min(set)

Returns the minimum value in the set.

```
>>> c
set([2, 3, 4, 5, 6, 7, 8, 9, 11])
>>> min(c)
2
```

max(set)

Returns the maximum value in the set.

```
>>> cset([2, 3, 4, 5, 6, 7, 8, 9, 11])
>>> max(c)
11
```

Set Methods

The following methods are available for sets.

.clear( )

Removes all data from the set.

```
>>> b = set([1,2,3,4,5])
>>> b
set([1, 2, 3, 4, 5])
>>> b.clear()
>>> b
set([])
```

.copy( )

Creates a new set by making a shallow copy.

```
>>> b
set([3, 4, 5, 6])
>>> c = b.copy()
>>> c
set([3, 4, 5, 6])
```

.pop( )

Removes an arbitrary item from the set. If the set is empty, a KeyError exception is raised.

```
>>> b = set([1,2,3,4,5])
>>> b
set([1, 2, 3, 4, 5])
>>> b.pop()
1
>>> b.pop()
2
>>> b.pop()
```

```
3
>>> b
set([4, 5])
```

.add(item)

Adds an item to the set. Since sets can not hold duplicates, if the item already exists, nothing will be done.

```
>>> b
set([4, 5])
>>> b.add(3)
>>> b
set([3, 4, 5])
>>> b.add(4)
>>> b
set([3, 4, 5])
```

.remove(item)

Deletes an item from the set. If the item does not exist, a KeyError exception will be raised.

```
>>> b
set([3, 4, 5])
>>> b.remove(4)
>>> b
set([3, 5])
>>> b.remove(4)
Traceback (most recent call last):
  File "<stdin>", line 1, in <module>
KeyError: 4
```

.discard(item)

Removes an item from the set. If the item is not in the set, no error will be raised.

```
>>> b
set([3, 5])
>>> b.discard(4)
>>> b.discard(5)
>>> b
set([3])
```

.update(set) or alternately x|=y

Merges values from the new set into the old set. If a value exists, it is ignored.

```
>>> b
set([3])
>>> b.update([3,2,1,4,5])
>>> b
set([1, 2, 3, 4, 5])
```

.intersection_update(set) or alternately x&=y

Updates the set x, discarading any elements that are not in both set x and y.

```
>>> a = set([1,2,3,4,5])
>>> b = set([2,3,4])
>>> a.intersection_update(b)
>>> a
set([2, 3, 4])
```

.difference_update(set) or alternately x-=y

Updates set x to a new set having only the values NOT in both set x and y.

```
>>> a = set([1,2,3,4,5])
>>> b = set([2,3,4])
>>> a.difference_update(b)
>>> a
set([1, 5])
```

.symmetric_difference_update(set) or alternately x^=y

Updates set x to contain only those values that are not in both set x and y.

```
>>> a = set([1,2,3])
>>> b = set([3,4,5])
>>> a.symmetric_difference_update(b)
>>> a
set([1, 2, 4, 5])
```

.issubset(set) or alternately x<=y

Returns True if set y is a subset of set x; otherwise, it returns False.

```
>>> a = set([1,2,3])
>>> b = set([3,4,5])
>>> c = set([2,3])
>>> c.issubset(a)
True
```

.issuperset(set) or alternately x>=y

Returns True if set x is a superset of set y; otherwise, it returns False.

```
>>> a = set([1,2,3])
>>> c = set([2,3])
>>> a.issubset(c)
True
```

.union(set) or alternately x|y

Returns a set that conains all unique values in sets x and y.

```
>>> a = set([1,2,3])
>>> c = set([5,6,7])
>>> a.union(c)
set([1, 2, 3, 5, 6, 7])
```

.intersection(set) or alternately x&y

Returns a new set that contains the values that are in both sets x and y.

```
>>> a
set([1, 2, 3])
>>> b
set([2, 3])
>>> a.intersection(b)
set([2, 3])
```

.difference(set) or alternately x-y

Returns a new set that contains the values that are not in both sets x and y.

```
>>> a
set([1, 2, 3])
>>> b
set([2, 3])
>>> a.difference(b)
set([1])
```

.symmetric_difference(set) or alternately x^y

Returns a new set that contains the values that are not in both sets x and y, but does not update set x.

```
>>> a
set([1, 2, 3])
>>> b = set([3,4,5])
>>> a.symmetric_difference(b)
set([1, 2, 4, 5])
```

Frozensets

Frozensets are, for the most part, the same as sets, except they are immutable (they can not be changed). This means that the .add and .update methods will return an error.

## CHAPTER 7

Keywords

Keywords are special reserved words that cannot be used as variable names. Keywords will change over time as Python versions change. Below is a short program that will allow you to obtain a list of keywords specific for your version of Python. It is written using Python 3.x syntax, but will work for version 2.7 as well.

```
Import keyword
print(keyword.kwlist)
```

List of Python Keywords

Below is a list of Python keywords, in alphabetical order, for version 2.7.1.

and	as	assert	break
class	continue	def	del
elif	else	except	exec
finally	for	from	global
if	import	in	is
lambda	not	or	pass
print	raise	return	try
while	with	yield	

In addition, Python 3.x adds four keywords and removes one. The additional keywords are:

False	None	True	nonlocal

The keyword exec has been removed from Python 3.x.

The list below is ordered by type.

Boolean	Conditional	Debugging	Error Handling	Evaluation
And	Elif	Assert	Except	In
Is	Else	Print	Finally	none
Not	If		Raise	
or	pass		try	
Functions	Iterators/ Generators	Libraries	Loops	Misc
Def	yield	As	Break	Class
Lambda		From	Continue	Del
Pass		import	For	exec
return			In	
			Pass	
			While	
Output	Unmanaged Resources	Variables		
print	with	Global		
		None		
		nonlocal		

Keywords Explained

Below we will examine each keyword, what it does and how it would be used. The keywords for Python 2.x are presented in alphabetical order for easy reference with the additional keywords for Python 3.x following. The following format will be used for each keyword:

- Keyword
- Used for or in
- Explanation and code (where appropriate)

and
Boolean Evaluation

The *and* keyword evaluates two equations, and if both are true then returns true. If either of the two are false, then returns false.

```
>>> a = 1
>>> b = 2
>>> a > 1 and b == 2
False
>>> b == 2 and a > 1
False
>>> a > 0 and b == 2
True
>>> a < b and b == 2
True
```

as
Libraries, Modules

Allows us to create a different reference name, or alias, for a module or function imported into our program.

```
>>> import sys as s
>>> print s.version
2.7.1 (r271:86832, Nov 27 2010, 18:30:46) [MSC v.1500 32 bit (Intel)]
```

assert
Debugging

The *assert* keyword forces a test of an expression and the compiler will error out if the expression is false.

```
>>> c = 3
>>> assert c<1
Traceback (most recent call last):
  File "<stdin>", line 1, in <module>
AssertionError
>>> assert c > 4
Traceback (most recent call last):
  File "<stdin>", line 1, in <module>
AssertionError
>>> assert c == 3
>>>
```

break
Loops

The *break* keyword allows the current loop to be aborted early. The following snippet shows that when the counter variable 'i' reaches 5, the loop will be exited.

```
for i in range(10):
    print i
    if i == 5:
        break
```

0
1
2
3
4
5

class
Misc.

The *class* keyword allows you to create a new class, which is important for Object Oriented Programming.

The class must be instantiated by assigning it to a variable. Then we can call any of the functions within the class.

```
class test1:
    def __init__(self,inval):
        self.a = inval #dummy statement

    def run(self):
        for cntr in range(self.a):
            print cntr

t = test1(20)
t.run()
```

continue
Conditional Statements, Loops

The *continue* keyword is used in loops to skip the rest of the code within the loop for that iteration of the loop. In the following snippet, notice that if the cntr variable hits the number 5, it will skip the print statement and continue back to the top of the loop.

```
for cntr in range(10):
    if cntr == 5:
        continue
    print cntr
```

```
0
1
2
3
4
6
7
8
9
```

def
Functions

The *def* keyword allows us to create a function.

```
def log(strng):
    print(strng)

log("This is a test...")
```

This is a test...

del
Misc

The *del* keyword removes a value or values from a list given its index.

```
>>> lst = [1,2,3,4,5,6]
>>> lst
[1, 2, 3, 4, 5, 6]
>>> del lst[3]
>>> lst
[1, 2, 3, 5, 6]
```

In the above example, we request that the item at index position 3, in list lst be deleted. Remember, all indexes are zero based, so that would be the number 4.

You can also delete items in a list using a slice. The command del lst[:2] would delete the first two items in the list, leaving (after the first *del* command) [3,5,6].

elif
Conditional Statements

The *elif* statement is an optional part of the *if* conditional statement. It is used when the expression(s) above it evaluate to False and you want to test other expressions. The *elif* statement is at the same indention level as the *if* statement line and is followed by an additional statement to be evaluated then by a colon. The code block must be indented. There can be as many *elif* statements as needed and may be followed by an *else* statement if desired (see below).

```
a = 3
if a == 1:
    print("Variable A = 1")
elif a == 2:
    print("Variable A = 2")
elif a == 3:
    print("Variable A = 3")
else:
    print("Variable is greater than 3")
```

else
Conditional Statements

The *else* keyword is an optional part of the *if* conditional statement. It is used when the if statement (or any elif statements) evaluates to false. This can be considered an "all else has failed, so do the following code." The *else* keyword is at the same indentation level as the *if* statement line and is followed immediately by a colon. No expressions are allowed on the line containing the *else* keyword. The logic block that needs to be executed is indented at the same level as the logic block for the main *if* statement. The *else* keyword is also an optional part of the *for* and *while* loops.

```
a = 3
if a > 5:
    print("Variable a is greater than 5")
else:
    print("Variable a is less than 5")
```

except
Error Handling

The *except* keyword is used with the try keyword for error trapping. If the code within the *try* block fails for any reason, the code within the *except* block will be executed. This code can be a simple *pass* statement, or something that logs or outputs the error information. There may also be several different *except* statements, each handling a specific error.

```
try:
    # try block code here
except:
    # except block code here
```

The except clause may contain some sort of test for the type of error that was encountered.

```
try:
    # try block code here
except TypeError:
    # except block code here
```

exec
Misc.

Executes Python statements that are stored in a string or a file. (version 2.x only). This could create a security problem and should only be used as a last resort.

```
>>> code = 'print "This is a test"'
>>> exec code
'print "This is a test"'
```

finally
Error Handling

The *finally* keyword is part of the *try / except* error handling system. The code in the *finally* block will be always be run leaving the try code block regardless of whether an error was encountered or not. This is a good place to put code that closes files or releases network resources.

```
try:
    # try block code here
except:
    # except block code here
finally:
    # finally block code here that will always run.
```

for
Loops

The *for* keyword creates a loop controlled by the parameters that follow the keyword Like the *if* statement the keyword is followed by a sequence (iterable such as a list or string) followed by a colon. All programming statements that are to be done within the loop is indented. In its simplest form the *for* loop looks like this:

```
for I in range(10):
    print(i)
```

More about *for* loops can be found in Chapter 5.

from
Libraries

The *from* keyword allows us to import a variable or function directly from a specific library module without having to qualify the library name (i.e., sys.path). It also imports only the requested routines from the library. If you wish to import all functions from a library you can use something like "import sys" or "from sys import *".

```
>>> from sys import path
>>> path
['', 'C:\\WINDOWS\\system32\\python27.zip', 'C:\\Python27\\DLLs',
'C:\\Python27\
\lib', 'C:\\Python27\\lib\\plat-win', 'C:\\Python27\\lib\\lib-tk',
'C:\\Python27
', 'C:\\Python27\\lib\\site-packages']
```

global
Variables

As I discussed in cCapter 2, variables have a limited scope. If a variable is declared within a function, any manipulation of that variable is limited to that code block within the function, even if the name of the variable is the same of one that is used outside of that function. The *global* keyword allows the manipulation to affect other variables outside of the scope of that routine.

```
x = 3
def tryit():
    global x
    x = 6
def tryit2():
    global x
    x = x * 3
>>> x
6
>>> tryit2()
>>> x
```

18
```
>>> tryit()
>>> x
```
6

if
Conditional Statements

The *if* keyword is used for conditional statements. In its simplest form, the *if* statement consists of an expression that gets evaluated at run time and a block of code (which can consist of single line) that will get executed at run time if the expression is true. The *if* statement can be extended by the *elif* and *else* keywords explained earlier. The format for the *if* statement starts with the *if* keyword, followed by the expression and a colon. The block of code that is to be executed if the expression is true must be indented. All indented code will be considered as part of the logic block. If the expression is not true, the code will pass to the next unindented line of code, which could be an elif, else or just the next line of the program code.

```
a = 3
if a > 2:
    print("Variable A is greater than 2")
```

import
Libraries

The *import* keyword allows code from outside libraries to be included in our code.

```
>>> import sys
>>> print(sys.version)
2.7.1 (r271:86832, Nov 27 2010, 18:30:46) [MSC v.1500 32 bit (Intel)]
```

in
Evaluation, Loops

The *in* keyword can be used to test the existence of a value within a tuple, list or other iterable.

```
>>> a = (1,2,3)
>>> 4 in a
False
>>> 3 in a
True
```

You can also use the in keyword as part of a *for* loop. In the following snippet, a list that contains the values from 0 to 9 is created by the "range" function and that list is iterated or walked to do the loop.

```
for i in range(10):
    print i,
```

0 1 2 3 4 5 6 7 8 9

is
Boolean Evaluation

The *is* keyword evaluates two expressions, checking to see if they are the same object. You can not evaluate two empty lists (x = [] and y = []) because they are not the same object.

```
>>> m = 2
>>> x = 2
>>> m is x
True
>>> m is 2
True
```

lambda
Functions

Allows the creation of an anonymous inline function.

```
>>> a = lambda d,e,f : d+e+f+3
>>> a(1,2,3)
9
>>> t = (lambda a='one',b='two',c='three' : a+b+c)
>>> t('four','five')
'fourfivethree'
```

not
Boolean Evaluation

The *not* keyword negates a Boolean value. True becomes False and False becomes True.

```
>>> a = 1
>>> b = 2
>>> not(a == b) # a==b is false. not(False) becomes True
True
```

or
Boolean Evaluation

Tests all expressions, and if at least one is True then returns True, otherwise returns False.

```
a = "Test"
b = "Of"
c = "OR"
if a == "1" or b == "Three" or c == "ORD":
    print("True")
else:
    print("False")
```

False

```
if a == "1" or b == "Three" or c == "OR":
    print("True")
else:
    print("False")
```

True

pass
Conditional Statements, Loops

The *pass* keyword allows you to "stub" out a function or conditional option that is not yet finished.

```
Def DummyFunction():
    pass

if a > 2:
    pass
else:
    pass
```

print
Output, Debugging

The *print* keyword allows you to send output to the terminal or command prompt during the execution of your code. When in the debugging stage of your program, you can also use the print keyword to display the value of certain variables to help you see where your code might be going wrong.

Python 2.x allows for the print statement to be formatted like this:

```
>>> x = 3
>>> y = 4
>>> print x,y
3 4
```

However, Python 3.x changes the print statement to a function, so it requires print to be formatted with parentheses surrounding the statement:

```
>>> x = 3
>>> y = 4
>>> print(x,y)
3 4
```

If you try to use the 2.x format in 3.x, you will get a syntax error. Python 2.x does allow the 3.x syntax, so you should use the 3.x format whenever possible when you write new code under Python 2.x.

The *print* keyword will normally add an escape sequence new line character ('\n') to the output unless a comma is placed at the end of the statement.

```
for x in range(10):
    print x,
```

```
0 1 2 3 4 5 6 7 8 9
```

For more information on escape sequences, see the Escape Sequence below.

raise
Error Handling

The *raise* keyword forces a specified error to occur. This is helpful for testing and debugging purposes.

```
y = 3
if y < 10:
    raise ValueError
Traceback (most recent call last):
  File "<stdin>", line 2, in <module>
ValueError
```

return
Functions

The *return* keyword will pass a value or values back to the line of code that called the function.

```
def returntest():
    a = 4
    b = 2
    return a * b

>>> print(returntest())
8
```

It is possible to return multiple values from a function. In this case, the return value is a tuple.

```
def returntest2():
    a = 4
    b = 2
    c = a * b
    return a,b,c
>>> print(returntest2())
(4, 2, 8)
```

try
Error Handling

The *try* keyword is part of a very versatile error handling system that Python provides. The *try* statement should always be used with a matching *except* statement. The general format looks something like this:

```
try:
    # code here to attempt to execute
except:
    # code here to attempt to recover from the error
```

The code between the *try* and *except* keywords is run. If no error occurs, the *except* portion of the routine is bypassed. If an error does occur, the code after the *except* keyword will be run. See also *except* and *finally,* above. There is also an optional *else* clause, which can contain code that will be executed if the *try* clause did not raise an error. The else clause must follow the *except* clause.

while
Loops

The *while* keyword creates a loop that is executed over and over until a condition becomes true.

```
cntr = 0
while cntr < 9:
```

```
    print cntr
    cntr += 1
0
1
2
3
4
5
6
7
8
```

with
Unmanaged resources

The *with* keyword allows you to deal with unmanaged resources, like files. If you need to quickly write to a file and make sure that it gets saved when the code is finished automatically, you can use the *with* keyword. In the snippet below, the *with* keyword opens the output file and then after the code below it is finished processing, it automatically closes the file for you.

```
with open('output.txt','w') as f:
    f.write('Welcome to Python')
```

yield
Iterators, Generators

Returns a generator. Generators are a simple and yet powerful tool for creating iterators. They are written like a regular function but use the yield statement whenever they want to return data. Each time next() is called, the generator resumes where it left off (it remembers all data values and which statement was last executed). In the code sample below, each time the loop executes, it automatically calls the next() statement.

```
def CreateGen():
    mylist = range(5)
    print mylist
    for i in mylist:
        yield i*i

mygen = CreateGen()
for cntr in mygen:
    print(cntr)
```

```
[0, 1, 2, 3, 4]
0
1
4
9
16
```

False
Evaluation (Version 3.x only)

In Python 2.x, *False* was simply a built-in constant. You were welcome to override it and, in fact, could write the following:

```
False = True
```

and it would be prefectly legal. In version 3.x it has been promoted to a keyword and is used to mean "0".

None
Evaluation, Variables (Version 3.x only)

The *None* keyword represents the concept of empty and nothing. If a variable has not been assigned a value it is automatically given a value of *None*. When a function is created that does not explicitly return a value, the function returns a *None* value.

```
>>> fred = None
>>> print fred
None
```

True
Evaluation (Version 3.x only)

In Python 2.x, *True* was simply a built-in constant. You were welcome to override it and, in fact, could write the following:

```
True = False
```

and it would be prefectly legal. In version 3.x it has been promoted to a keyword and is used to mean "not 0".

nonlocal
Variables (Version 3.x only)

Similar to the *global* keyword but is only relevant within a function. Functions may have nested functions. Without the *nonlocal* keyword, any declared variables have the scope of a normal function, even if they are nested within another function. By using the *nonlocal* keyword within the nested function, the variable value may be changed within the nested routine. In the following example, there are two functions, each with a nested function. The two functions are identical with the exception of the *nonlocal* keyword in Funct1. The variable test in Funct2 has a local scope within the Within function, so the outer variable test is not changed. In Funct1, however, it is set as a *nonlocal* variable, so that the outer variable test gets modified by the Within function nested in Funct1.

```
def Funct1():
    test = 1
    def Within():
        nonlocal test
        test = 2
        print("Routine Funct1|Within- test = ", test)
    Within()
    Print("Routine Funct1 - test = ", test)

def Funct2():
    test = 1
    def Within():
        test = 2
        print("Routine Funct2|Within - test = ", test)
    Within()
    print("Routine Funct2 - test = ",test)

Funct2()
Funct1()
```

```
Routine Funct2|Within - test = 2
Routine Funct2 - test = 1
Routine Funct1|Within- test = 2
Routine Funct1 - test = 2
```

Escape Sequences

Python allows for certain characters such as a Tab or Carriage Return to be embedded within strings to allow extra control over printing. There are also times that you have a string that requires a single or double quote that would normally cause problems. For example, let's say you decided to create a string using the single quote as the string delimiter. Without using an escape sequence you can't have a single quote within the string. While you could use double quotes to delimit the string, that might be an issue.

```
>>> test = 'This is a test of the \' (single quote) character'
>>> test
```
"This is a test of the ' (single quote) character"

The escape sequence starts with a backslash (\) character then followed by a character. This will be interpreted by Python as a special character. Refer to Table 7-1.

Table 7-1. *List of Escape Sequences*

Escape Sequence	Meaning
\\	Backslash (\)
\'	Single Quote (')
\"	Double Quote (")
\a	ASCII Bell (BEL)
\b	ASCII Backspace (BS)
\f	ASCII Formfeed (FF)
\n	ASCII Linefeed (LF)
\N	Character named *name* in the Unicode database
\r	ASCII Charriage Return (CR)
\t	ASCII Horizontal Tab (TAB)
\uxxxx	Character with 16-bit hex value (Unicode only)
\Uxxxxxxxx	Character with 32 bit hex value (Unicode only)
\v	ASCII Vertical Tab(VT)
\ooo	Charcter with octal value ooo
\xhh	Character with hex value hh

CHAPTER 8

Functions

We have already shown the functions that are built into Python. Although there is a wealth of functions available to us, there will be times that you need to create your own. In some other programming languages, functions are known as subroutines.

There are usually two reasons for functions. The first is to organize the code into a logical way to handle certain tasks. The other is to be able to reuse code. The general rule of thumb is that if you have a block of code that gets called more than once, put it in a function.

Structure of a Function

The structure of a function is very simple but very important.

```
def {FunctionName}[(parameters)]: # Function Header
  Indented code..... # Code begins here
```

The header of a function defines the way it will be called. The header begins with the def keyword followed by the function name, then the optional parameter list and a colon. Even if there are no parameters, you must place parenthesis before the colon (e.g., def Toad( ):). All code for the function must be indented. The function name must follow the same naming rules for variables (Single word, No spaces, must start with either a letter or an underscore, etc). The optional parameter list contains variable names (preferably not used anywhere else) seperated by commas. The header ends at the colon.

The next line begins the function code and must be indented.

```
def CountUp(HowHigh):
  for Cntr in range(1,HowHigh+1):
    print(Cntr)
```

In this case, the function name is CountUp and there is one parameter, HowHigh. Notice that we don't have to declare what the type is for the parameter; it will be determined by the interpreter. Our code has just two lines, a **for** loop and a print statement.

Some people who have experience with other programming languages might say that this is a procedure, not a function, because it doesn't return anything. In some other programming languages, this might be true, but not in Python. In a case such as this, the function actually does return something, the None value.

Returning values

There will be times that your function needs to return one or more values. We use the return keyword to do this.

In the following example, we define a function called TestFunction that takes two values. The code simply returns the values back to the calling line. When we call the function, we assign two variables (a and b) to hold the two returned values.

```
def TestFunction(val1,val2):
    return val1,val2

a,b = TestFunction(3,2)
print('Returned from function... a = %d, b = %d' % (a,b))
```

Returned from function... a = 3, b = 2

Optional Parameters

Sometimes you need to provide for the possibility of optional parameters. For example, you want to add functionality if a second value is provided. Many times this could be a flag for the code. We do this by assigning a default value for that parameter. In the following code snippet, we define a function with a required parameter (val1) and an optional parameter (val2), which is assigned 0 as its default value. If the function is called with one parameter value, val2 will default to 0. One word of caution about using optional or default parameters: They are evaluated when the function is defined, not when the program is run. In the following example, we are safe because we are using a default of 0. However, if you set a default value for a parameter that is the result of another function (such as a time), it could cause great heartache and make you beat your head upon the keyboard for hours.

```
def TestFunction2(val1, val2=0):
    print('Required value = %d' % val1)
    if val2 != 0: # Only print the line below if val2 was provided
        print('Optional value = %d' % val2)

TestFunction2(1) # call function with only one value
print('')
TestFunction2(1,2) # call function with two values
```

Required value = 1

Required value = 1
Optional value = 2

You might realize that if val2 was passed a 0, the second line would not print. You can get around this issue by setting the default value for val2 to be None, as this code shows.

```
def TestFunction2(val1, val2=None):
    print('Required value = %d' % val1)
    if val2 != None:
        print('Optional value = %d' % val2)

TestFunction2(1)
print('')
TestFunction2(1,0)
```

Variables in and out of Functions

Where and how variables are defined determines when they may be changed. If we define a variable within a function or pass a value to a function, the value of that variable is only really accessable within that function. This is called scope.When we pass a variable to a function, what actually is passed is a reference to that variable.

Example 1

```
a = 5
def test(a):
    print('A = %d' % a)
    a += 10
    print('A is now %d' % a)

print('A starts with %d' % a)
test(a)
print('After test function a = %d' % a)
```

Here's what the program is supposed to do followed by its output.

1. Define a variable called 'a' and assign it to a value of 5.

2. Define a function called test that takes a parameter also called 'a'. Note that this is not the same variable.

3. Once we are in the function, we print the value of a (an assumption that 'a' is a decimal number is made here).

4. Add 10 to that value and print the new value. That is the end of the function and we do not return any values.

5. The program actually starts with the first line (a = 5) then skips the function and continues with the next nonindented line ('print('A starts...'). So we assign 5 to variable a, then we print "A starts with 5".

6. Call the function test with the variable a, which is 5, as the parameter.

7. Inside the function, we print "A = 5", then add 10 to it and print "A is now 15". When we exit the routine, we then print "After test function a = " and the value of 'a'.

Output

A starts with 5
A = 5
A is now 15
After test function a = 5

If you are surprised by this, you have to remember two things. The variable 'a' was defined outside of the function, and even though we changed the value passed in to 15, that value is strictly local to the function. We didn't actually change 'a'.

This could be looked at as a double edged sword. On the one hand, the value in any variable passed to a function is safe from manipulation. On the other hand, sometimes we actually need to change that value.

Example 2

There are two ways to change the value. The first way is to use the global keyword within the function. The second is to return a value.

Using Global Keyword

```
a = 1
def test1():
    a = 42
    print('Inside test1...a = %d' % a)

def test2():
    global a
    a = a + 1
    print('Inside test2...a = %d' % a)
print('a starts at %d' % a)
test1()
print('After test1, a is now %d' % a)
test2()
print('After test2, a is now %d' % a)
```

1. First we define a variable 'a' and assign the value of 1 to it.

2. Next we define two functions, test1 and test2. Neither of them will take a parameter

3. In the test1 function, we assign a variable 'a' and assign the value of 42 to it and print the value. Remember that this variable 'a' has a different scope which is strictly only for use within this function.

4. In test2, we use the global keyword when we define the variable 'a'. This time, because we used the global keyword, we are saying that anytime we use the variable 'a', it should refer to the global variable, not a local one. Now anything that happens to the variable 'a' within the routine will change the one declared in the first line of code.

5. Now the code continues and will print "a starts at 1", procedes to call fuction test1, which creates its own variable 'a', assigns the value of 42 to it and does the print.

6. When we come back from that, we print "After test1, a is now 1".

7. The function test2 is called next. Because we have declared that the variable 'a' in the function is the global one, it gets changed to 2 and we do the print, then on return from the function, we get "After test2, a is now 2".

Output

```
a starts at 1
Inside test1...a = 42
After test1, a is now 1
Inside test2...a = 2
After test2, a is now 2
```

Return a Value

Here is the same program we used earlier but modified to return the changed variable.

```
a = 5
def test(a):
    print('A = %d' % a)
    a += 10
    print('A is now %d' % a)
    return a
```

```
print('A starts with %d' % a)
a = test(a)
print('After test function a = %d' % a)
```

1. You can see that we only added one line (the "return a" line and modified the call to the test function by assigning the variable to pick up the return value.

2. When this program runs ... we assign 5 to variable 'a', pass it to the test function.

3. It prints the value that was just passed in, increments it by 10, prints the new value (15) and then returns the new value, which is received by the call to the function and changes the value 'a' from 5 to 15.

Output

```
A starts with 5
A = 5
A is now 15
After test function a = 15
```

Anatomy of a Python Program

Let's review the structure and an actual example.

Structure of a simple program

A simple python program has the following structure:

```
Shared Variable Declarations
Functions
Main Routine
```

A real example

So it would look something like this:

```
a = 24
b = 42
```

```
def function1(varA,varB):
    print(varA,varB)

def main():
    function1(a,b)

#...

main()
```

In this program example:

1. We declare variables 'a' and 'b' so that they are global in scope.

2. Next we declare two functions, one called 'function1' and one called 'main'.

3. The comment line with the elipses simply shows that there may be more functions below that.

4. The last line calls the function 'main' to start the program.

The exception to this generic template would be if we are writing a program that includes classes, which are discussed in detail in Chapter 10.

CHAPTER 9

Libraries

There are a tremendous number of libraries that are available for Python, both that come with the standard installation and available from the web. In this chapter, I will try to give you a list of some of the more "generically" helpful ones. Most of this information was obtained from the official Python Docs page.

String Services

Thes libraries provide various tools for dealing with string formatting, regular expressions, strings as files, Unicode strings, and more.

string—Common string operations

The string library contains a number of useful constants and classes, as well as some deprecated legacy functions that are also available as methods on strings.

re—Regular expression operations

The re library provides regular expression matching operations similar to those found in the Perl language. Both patterns and strings to be searched can be Unicode strings as well as 8-bit strings.

StringIO—Read and write strings as files

The StringIO library implements a filelike class that reads and writes a string buffer or memory files (2.x only).

Data Types

These libraries provide specialized data types such as dates and times, fixed type arrays, queues, and sets.

datetime—Basic date and time types

Includes objects such as time, date, timezone, and formatted time/date information.

sets—Extends the set capabilities of Python

Provides classes for constructing and manipulating unordered collections.

pprint—Data pretty printer

Provides the ability to "pretty print" data.

Numeric and Mathematical Librarys

Provides numeric and math-related function and data types.

numbers—Numeric abstract base cass

Defines a hierarchy of numeric base classes.

decimal—Decimal fixed point and floating point arithmetic

Offers serveral advantages over the normal 'float' datatype.

math—Mathematical functions

Provides functions such as floor, ceil, trigonometric functions, and more.

random—Generate pseudo-random numbers

The random library also provides shuffleing, random sampling functions, and more.

File and Directory Access

Provides libraries for dealing with disk files and directories.

os.path—Common pathname manipulations

Implements useful functions on pathnames.

fileinput—iterate over lines from input streams

Provides helper class and functions to quickly write a loop over standard input or a list of files.

Data Persistance

Supports storing Python data in a persistent form on disk.

pickle—Python object serialization

Implements powerful algorithm for serializing and deserializing a Python object structure.

anydbm—Generic access to DBM-style databases

Generic interface to varients of the DBM database. This library has been renamed to dbm in Python 3.x.

sqlite3—API interface for SQLite databases

Provides a SQL interface to SQLite databases.

Data Compression and Archiving

Supports data compression with zlib, gzip, bzip2 algorithms, and createion of ZIP and tar format archives.

zlib—Compression compatible with gzip

Allows compression and decompression of archives using the zlib library.

gzip—Support for gzip files

Simple interface to compress and decompress files such as the gzip and gunzip programs.

bz2—Compression compatible with bzip2

Provides a comprehensive interface for the bz2 compression library.

zipfile—Work with ZIP archives

Provides tools to create, read, write, append, and list ZIP files.

File Formats

These libraries parse various miscellaneous file formats that aren't markup languages or related to e-mail.

csv—CSV File Reading and Writing

Implements classes to read and write tabular data is CSV (Comma Seperated Variable) files.

ConfigParser—Configuration file Parser

Implements a basic configuration file parser language, which provides a structure similar to Microsoft Windows INI files. This library has been renamed to configparser in Python 3.x.

Cryptographic Services

This set of library modules implements various algorithms of a cryptographic nature.

hashlib—Secure hashes and message digest algorithm

Implements a common interface to many different secure hash and message algorithms.

md5—MD5 message digest algorithm

Implements an interface to RSA's MD5 algorithm.

sha—SHA-1 message digest algorithm

Implements an interface to NIST's Secure Hash Algorithm.

Generic Operating System Services

There are many libraries in this section that provide interfaces to operating system features.

os—Miscellaneous operating system interfaces.

This library provides a portable way of using operating dependent functionality. Provides functions such as chdir, getenv, file open, and file close.

io—Core tools for working with streams

Provides a Python interface to stream handling.

time—Time access and conversions

Provides various time-related functions.

argparse—Parser for commandline options, arguments, and subcommands

Provides an easy method to write command-line interface processing.

curses—Terminal handling for character displays

Provides an interface to the curses library for portable advanced terminal handling. Provides functions such as colored text, positional printing, and screen clearing in a terminal or command window.

logging—Logging library for Python

The logging library provides functions and classes that implement a flexible event logging system. Very useful for debugging.

Optional Operating system Services

Provides interfaces to operating system features that are generally modeled after Unix interfaces.

threading

Provides higher-level threading interfaces.

Multiprocessing—Process-based "threading" interface

Provides support for spawing processing using an API similar to the threading library.

readline—GNU readline interface

Provides a number of functions to facilitate completion and reading/writing history files.

Interprocess Communication and Networking

socket—Low-level networking interface

Provides access to the BSD socket interface.

ssl—TLS/SSL wrapper for socket objects

Provides access to Transport Layer Security (Secure Sockets Layer) encryption for network sockets.

popen2—Subprocesses with accessible I/O streams

Provides routines to spawn processes and connect to the IO pipes under Unix and Windows.

Internet Data Handling

Provides librarys that support handling data formats commonly used on the Internet.

email—An e-mail and MIME handling package

Library for managing e-mail messages.

json—lightweight data interchange format based on a subset of JavaScript

exposes an API familiar to users of marshal and pickle librarys.

uu—Encode and decode uuencoded files

Provides the ability to encode and decode uuencode format files.

Structured Markup Processing Tools

Provides support for working with various forms of structured data markup.

HTMLParser—Simple HTML and XHTML parser

Provides basis for parsing text files formatted in HTML and XHTML. HTMLParser has been renamed to html.parser in Python 3.x.

htmllib—Parser for HTML documents

Provides a class that allows for parsing text files formatted in HTML. Removed in Python 3.

xml.etree.elementtree—ElementTree XML API

Provides a flexable container object that handles XML files.

xml.dom—The Document Object Module API

Provides an easy way to handls DOM XML files.

xml.sax—Support for SAX2 parsers

Provides a number of librarys for SAX.

Internet Protocols and support

Provides libraries that implement Internet protocols and support for related technology.

webbrowser—Convienient Web-browser controller

Provides a high-level interface to allow displaying Web-based documents to users.

cgi—Common Gateway Interface support

Support library for Common Gateway Interface (CGI) scripts.

urllib—Open arbitrary resources by URL

Provides a high-level interface for fetching data across the World Wide Web. Has been split into parts and renamed in Python 3, named urllib.request, urllib.parse, and urllib.error. urllib.urlopen() function has been removed in Python 3.x in favor of urllib2.urlopen().

urllib2—extensible library for opening URSs

Provides functions and classes that help opening URLs. Has been split across several modules in Python 3 named urllib.request and urllib.error.

poplib—POP3 protocol client

Provides a class that allows connection to POP3 servers.

Multimedia Services

Implements various algorithms or interfaces that are useful for multimedia applications.

audioop—Manipulate raw audio data

Provides useful routines for sound fragments.

wave—Read and write WAV files

Provides a convenient interface to the WAV sound format.

Internationalization

Provides libraries that are independent of language and locale.

gettext—Multilngual internationalization services

Provides internationalization and localization services with an API.

locale—Internationalization services

Provides access to the POSIX local database and functionality.

Program Frameworks

This set of libraries are frameworks that are oriented toward writing command-line interfaces.

Cmd—Support for line-oriented command interpreters

Provides a simple framework for writing line-oriented command intrepers. These are often useful for test harnesses, administrative tools, and prototypes.

shlex—Simple lexical analysis

The shlex class makes it easy to write lexical analyzers for simple syntaxes resembling that of the Unix shell.

Graphical User Interfaces with Tk

Tk/Tcl has long been an integral part of Python. It provides a robust and platform independent windowing toolkit.

Tkinter—Python interface to Tcl/Tk

The Tkinter library is the standard Python to the Tk GUI toolkit.

ttk—Tk-themed widgets

The ttk library provides access to the Tk-themed widget set.

turtle—Turtle graphics for Tk

Turtle graphics is a popular way for introducing programming to kids. It was part of the original Logo programming language developed in 1966 by Wally Feurzig and Seymour Papert.

Development Tools

pydoc—Documentation generator and online help system

Automatically generates documentation from Python librarys. The documentation can be presented as pages of text in a terminal or command window or saved to HTML files.

unittest—Unit testing framework

Supports test automation, aggregation tests into collections.

2to3—Automated Python 2 to Python 3 code translation

A Python program that reads Python 2.x source code and applies a series of "fixers" to transfer it into a valid Python 3.x code set.

Debugging and Profiling

The libraries in this section helps with Python development. The debugger enables you to step through code, analyze stack frames and set breakpoints, and so on.

pdb—The Python Debugger

This library defines an interactive source code debugger for Python programs. It supports setting breakpoints and single stepping at the source line level.

hotshot—High performance logging profiler

This library provides a nicer interface to the _hotshot C library.

timeit—Measure execution time of small code snippets

This library provides a simple way to time small bits of Python code.

trace—Trace or track Python statement execution

This library allows you to trace program execution, generate annotated statement coverage listings, print caller/callee relationships and list functions executed during a program run.

Python Runtime Services

These libraries provide a wide range of services related to the Python interpreter and its interaction with its environment.

sys—System-specific parameters and functions

This library provides access to variables and functions that interact with the interpreter.

warnings—Warning control

Supports the use of warning messages in situations in which it is useful to alert the user of some condition in a program where that condition normally doesn't warrant raising an exception and terminating the program.

Custom Python Interpreters

Libraries in this section allow for writing interfaces similar to Pythons interactive interpreter.

codeop

Provides utilities on which the Python read-eval-print loop can be emulated.

code—Interpreter base classes

Provides facilities to implement read-eval-print loops in Python.

Importing Librarys

These libraries provide new ways to import other Python librarys and hooks for customizing the import process.

zipimport—Import librarys from Zip archives

Adds the ability to import Python librarys and packages from Zip format archives.

runpy—Locating and executing Python librarys

This library is used to locate and run Python librarys without importing them first.

Python Language Services

Libraries that assist in working with the Python language.

Parser—Access Python parse trees

This library provides an interface to Python's internal parser and byte-code compiler.

tabnanny—Detection of ambiguous indentation.

This library is intended to be called as a script to check whitespace in a source file.

MS Windows Specific Services

These libraries are only available on MS Windows platforms.

msilib—Read and write Microsoft installer files

Supports creation of Microsoft Installer (.msi) files.

_winreg—Windows registry access

This library exposes the Windows registry API to Python.

winsound—Sound playing interface for Windows

Provides access to the basic sound-playing functions provided by the Windows platforms.

Unix Specific Services

These libraries provide interfaces to features that are unique to Unix operating system.

posix—The most common POSIX system calls

This library provides access to operating system functionality that is standardized by the C Standard and the POSIX standard. Do not import this library directly. Instead, import the *os* library which provides a portable version of this interface.

pwd—The password database

This library provides access to the Unix user account and password database.

tty -Terminal control functions

This library defines functions for putting the tty into cbrake and raw modes.

Mac OS X

Thes libraries are only available on the Mac OS X platform. Many of these libraries are not available when Python is executing in 64-bit mode and have been removed in Python 3.x.

MacOs—Access to Mac OS interpreter fetures

This library provides access to MacOS specific functionality in the Python interpreter. Has been removed in Python 3.x.

Easy Dialogs—Basic Macintosh dialogs

Contains simple dialogs for the Macintosh. This library has been removed in Python 3.x.

MacPython OSA Librarys

These libraries support implementation of the Open Scripting Architecture (OSA) for Python.

aetools—OSA Client support

This library contains the basic functionality for the Python AppleScript client. Removed in Python 3.x.

Aepack—Conversion between Python variables and AppleEvent data containers

This library defines functions for converting Python variables to AppleEvent and back. Removed in Python 3.x.

SGI IRIX Specific Services

Libries providing features unique to SGI's IRIX operating system versions 4 and 5.

gl—Graphics library interface

Provides access to the Silicon Graphics Graphics library. It is only available on SGI machines and has been removed in Python 3.x.

al—Audio functions on the SGI

Provides access to the audio facilities of the SGI Indy and Indigo workstations. Has been removed in Python 3.x.

SunOS Specific Services

Provides libraries that are specific to SunOS 5 (aka Solaris version 2).

sunaudiodev—Access to Sun audio hardware

Provides access to the Sun audio interface. Has been removed in Python 3.x.

■ ■ ■

## CHAPTER 10

Classes

Classes are the way that we create objects. We use objects to try to model the real world in computer code. Objects are a way of encapsulating programming code that, not only can be reusable, but can be duplicated and modified without affecting the original object. Objects often have attributes and functions to modify those attributes. Classes also allow you to write a group of code that may be used in multiple projects without rewriting or copying the code into each project just like a library. We will concentrate on objects in this chapter, all though the concepts are the same for simple classes.

What is an object?

When trying to explain what objects are, I like to use the example of a car. What is a car? It's a thing that has a body, a frame, an engine, a number of wheels, and more. The body type, the frame type, the engine type, the number of wheels, the color of the body, and other things are all examples of the attributes of the car. All cars have, for example, doors. However, the number of doors can change from model to model of cars. Some have two doors, some four, and some five (if you consider a trunk lid a door). We can create a "generic" car (called an instance) and then for whatever type of car we want, we can modify the attributes of that instance of a car to suit our own purposes. This is called inheritance. The new "model" of car we create by modifying the attributes, inherit the attributes of the parent.

Creating a Class

When we create a class, we use a class definition, very similar to a function definition. The class definition starts at the first position on the line with the word 'class' and ends with a colon. Any code lines within the class are indented. The first unindented line in code is considered outside of (not part of) the class.

```
class ClassName:
    {Any accessable class variables}
    {initialization routine}
    {Any functions you may need}
    ...
```

Here is an example:

```
class Car:
    __init__(self,attrib1,attrib2):
        pass

    def Function1(self):
        pass

     def Function2(self):
         pass
```

This is all fairly self-explanitory, with the possible exception of the word "self" in each of the definitions of the functions. The word "self" refers to the fact that we are using a variable or function within the specific instance of the class or object.

An Actual Example

Let's look at an example of a class and an object created by that class. We will create a class called "Dog". The class will have the following attributes:

- name (dogname)
- color (dogcolor)
- height (dogheight)
- build (dogbuild)
- mood (dogmood)
- age (dogage)

```
class Dog(): # The class definition
    def __init__(self,dogname,dogcolor,dogheight,dogbuild,dogmood,dogage):
        #here we setup the attributes of our dog
        self.name = dogname
        self.color = dogcolor
        self.height = dogheight
        self.build = dogbuild
        self.mood = dogmood
        self.age = dogage
        self.Hungry = False
        self.Tired = False
```

Most classes (and object) have an initialization function. This is **automatically** run when we create an instance of the class. To define the initialization routine, we name it __init__ (that's two underscore characters, followed by the word "**init**" followed by two more underscores) and then the parameter list, if any, and finally a colon just like any function we would normally write.

Within the initialization routine, we set up and define any internal variables or in this case attributes. Notice that we are also defining two attribute variables called Hungry and Tired that are not part of the parameter list. Normally, we would not "expose" or reveal these to the outside world and would only allow the internal functions to change them. In order to have variables or attributes hidden from the users of our objects, we start the variable name with two underscore characters. An example would be __Hungry and __Tired. However, because we are keeping things simple, we will expose everthing.

The functions within our class

Within the class we write functions just like any other function. We start the parameter list with the self keyword. If you don't use the self keyword, you will get some weird errors. When we refer to any of the internal variables, we use the .self keyword. The following three funtions are used to "tell the dog object what to do". Of course there could be many more, but for this example, we'll stick with these.

```
def Eat(self):
    if self.Hungry:
        print 'Yum Yum...Num Num'
        self.Hungry = False
    else:
        print 'Sniff Sniff...Not Hungry'

def Sleep(self):
    print 'ZZZZZZZZZZZZZZZZZZZZZZZZZZZZZZZZ'
    self.Tired = False

def Bark(self):
    if self.mood == 'Grumpy':
        print 'GRRRRR...Woof Woof'
    elif self.mood == 'Laid Back':
        print 'Yawn...ok...Woof'
    elif self.mood == 'Crazy':
        print 'Bark Bark Bark Bark Bark Bark Bark'
    else:
        print 'Woof Woof'
```

You can see that the code for these three functions is extremely simple.

The Eat function simply checks the Hungry attribute. If Hungry is True, then the dog object "eats" and then sets the attribute to False. If not, it just prints its line.

The Sleep function simply prints snores and then sets the 'Tired' attribute to False.

The Bark function walks through an if/elif/else statement and, based on the mood attribute, prints something appropriate.

Using the dog object

The following line of code will create an instance of the class/object (also called *instantiation*) and passes the correct information to the class initialization function, if there is one. Notice that this is part of the "main" code, not part of the class.

```
Beagle = Dog('Archie','Brown','Short','Chubby','Grumpy',12)
```

We now have a dog object called "Beagle". As you can see, he's (it's probably a he because the name is Archie) brown, short, chubby, and grumpy. Now we use the object. To access any of his functions or attributes, we use the object name (Beagle) followed by a dot (.) and then the function name or attribute name.

In the next five lines of code, we are accessing his attributes.

```
print 'My name is %s' % Beagle.name
print 'My color is %s' % Beagle.color
print 'My mood is %s' % Beagle.mood
print 'I am hungry = %s' % Beagle.Hungry
```

The last four lines of code will have him do things or, in the case of the second line, make him hungry.

```
Beagle.Eat()
Beagle.Hungry = True
Beagle.Eat()
Beagle.Bark()
```

When we run this program, we get the following output:

```
My name is Archie
My color is Brown
My mood is Grumpy
I am hungry = False
Sniff Sniff...Not Hungry
Yum Yum...Num Num
GRRRRR...Woof Woof
```

Going Further

We can extend this example by creating multiple instances of the Dog class. After the line that we initialize the Beagle object, replace all the following lines of code with these lines:

```
Lab = Dog('Nina','Black','Medium','Chubby','Laid Back',8)
Shepherd = Dog('Bear','Black','Big','Skinny','Crazy',14)
Lab.Hungry = True
print 'My name is %s' % Beagle.name
print 'My color is %s' % Beagle.color
print 'My mood is %s' % Beagle.mood
print 'I am hungry = %s' % Beagle.Hungry
Beagle.Eat()
Beagle.Hungry = True
Beagle.Eat()
Beagle.Bark()
print 'My name is %s' % Lab.name
print 'My mood is %s' % Lab.mood
if Lab.Hungry == True:
    print 'I am starving!'
    Lab.Eat()
    Lab.Sleep()
    Lab.Bark()
else:
    print 'No...not hungry.'
```

This creates two more Dog objects. One is called Lab and the other Shepherd, which along with the Beagle object, makes three. Running the code results in the following output:

```
My name is Archie
My color is Brown
My mood is Grumpy
I am hungry = False
Sniff Sniff...Not Hungry
Yum Yum...Num Num
GRRRRR...Woof Woof
My name is Nina
My mood is Laid Back
I am starving!
Yum Yum...Num Num
ZZZZZZZZZZZZZZZZZZZZZZZZZZZZZZZZZZZ
Yawn...ok...Woof
```

Obviously, there is much more you could do with this example. However, we will move on.

Something Real

Now we'll concentrate on something that is useful. We'll create a class that queries the WeatherUnderground website and get the current weather conditions for any given location in the United States by using the Zip Code. Before we go any further, let's layout a series of requirements for the class:

- Gets the current weather conditions

- Gets the Current Temp

- Gets the Current Barometric Pressure

- Gets the Relative Humidity

- Gets the Current Wind direction and speed.

- Runs in a Command Window (Windows) or Terminal (Linux)

Now we should look at the process that the program will perform:

1. Get the Zip code.

2. Instantiate the class, pass the Zip code to the class.

3. Open a socket to the URL of the website and get the information in the form of an XML file.

4. Parse the returned XML file pulling the information we need.

5. Print the information from the parse process.

Before we can code, we need to know what information the website will give us.

Reviewing the Information

The XML file is too large to print here, so I will just give a partial dump of the XML data. The elipses denote that there is more data that has been cut for the sake of brevity.

```
<current_observation>
    <credit>Weather Underground NOAA Weather Station</credit>
    <credit_URL>http://wunderground.com/</credit_URL>
    ...
    <display_location>
        <full>Aurora, CO</full>
        <city>Aurora</city>
        <state>CO</state>
        <state_name>Colorado</state_name>
        <country>US</country>
    ...
    </display_location>
    <observation_location>
```

```
    <full>Aurora, Colorado</full>
    <city>Aurora</city>
    <state>Colorado</state>
    <country>US</country>
    ...
</observation_location>
<station_id>KBKF</station_id>
<observation_time>Last Updated on November 14, 12:55 PM MST
</observation_time>
    ...
<weather>Partly Cloudy</weather>
<temperature_string>54 F (12 C)</temperature_string>
<temp_f>54</temp_f>
<temp_c>12</temp_c>
<relative_humidity>41%</relative_humidity>
<wind_string>From the SSW at 5 MPH </wind_string>
<wind_dir>SSW</wind_dir>
<wind_degrees>200</wind_degrees>
    ...
</current_observation>
```

As you can see, there is a huge amount of information given to us and much of it we won't use. The items of interest are:

1. <full> for the location text.

2. <observation_time> for the time of the readings.

3. <weather> for the current conditions (partly cloudy, clear, etc.).

4. <temperature_string> for the temperature.

5. <relative_humidity> for the humidity.

6. <wind_string> for the wind direction and speed.

7. <pressure_string> for the barometric pressure.

If you are not familiar with XML data, I'll give you a VERY quick tutorial.

XML Refresher

XML is one of a number of markup languages that are based on HTML. XML works on the concept of tags, text and attributes. A tag works like the key in the dictionary key/value pairs (see Chapter 6) and the text is the value of the pair. If there is data for a tag, there will be an opening tag and a closing tag. The closing tag is exactly the same as the opening tag except it will start with a slash. It will look like this:

```
<tag>text</tag>
```

Where the </tag> is the end tag. An attribute is something that is part of the tag and contains extra information. In what we are dealing with in this code, we don't have to worry about attributes in an XML file. In the above example data, when we look for the <weather> information, we are looking for the tag <weather> and the text is 'Partly Cloudy.'

Time to Code . . .

Now that we know what we are looking for, we can start our coding.

Import the Libraries

We will start by importing the libraries that we need:

```
from xml.etree import ElementTree as ET
import urllib
import sys
```

All three libraries are standard libraries that come with the normal Python distribution.

Create the Class

Next we need to create our class. It will be named 'CurrentInfo' and will contain three functions. In order, they are:

- getCurrents—Does the web access and parsing of the XML data
- output—does the printing to the terminal window.
- DoIt—calls the above functions in the proper order.

Although I stated earlier that most classes have an initialization function, this class won't have one, because in this case there is really nothing to initialize. We'll start with our class definition and the first function:

```
class CurrentInfo:
    def getCurrents(self,debuglevel,Location):
```

There are three parameters for the getCurrents function. The self parameter won't take an argument or data. The debuglevel is either a 0 or 1 and is there to be a flag to print debugging information or not. Location is where the Zip code is passed into the function. Next, we check to see if the debug mode is turned on and if so, we print the location Zip code that was passed into the function:

```
        if debuglevel > 0:
            print "Location = %s" % Location
```

Connect to the Website

Next we attempt to connect to the WeatherUnderground website to get the XML data. We do this using the try/except error handling set. This is in case we have no Internet connection or the website doesn't respond in a timely manner. After the try keyword, we set the variable called CurrentConditions to the website URL and include the Zip code at the end:

```
try:
    CurrentConditions = _ 'http://api.wunderground.com/auto/wui/geo/
WXCurrentObXML/index.xml?query=%s' % Location
```

Now we set the default timeout for the connection to 8 seconds, and open a socket to the URL we set up using the CurrentConditions variable. If there is no error, we tell the XML parsing routine to grab the XML data from the socket, and then we close the socket:

```
urllib.socket.setdefaulttimeout(8)
usock = urllib.urlopen(CurrentConditions)
tree = ET.parse(usock)
usock.close()
```

If there was an error, then we print an error message to the terminal window, and if the debug mode is set to True, we print the location and use the exit routine from the sys library to terminate the program. The number 1 in the sys.exit(1) line says that there was an error that caused us to terminate early. Usually the code 0 means everything worked well, code 1 means "something weird happened," and 2 means a command line error occurred.

```
except:
    print 'ERROR - Current Conditions - Could not get information
from server...'
    if debuglevel > 0:
        print Location
        sys.exit(1)
```

Now, we are assuming that everything has worked correctly and the parser has gotten the XML data. I'm going to explain the first two parsing commands because all of them are the same except what we are looking for and the variables we assign the data to.

The getCurrents function

The first line (for loc in tree.findall(".//full":) tells the XML parser to look for the tag named *<full>*. Every tag with that name is pulled into a list named 'loc'. For each and every item in the list, we assign that item text to the self.location variable. In the case of this data, there are many *<full>* tags, but they all hold the same data. In the next one, we want to get the observation time. Just in case there is more than one instance, we use a *for* loop to assign the text to the self.obtime variable. Here is the code for this section:

```python
# Get Display Location
for loc in tree.findall(".//full"):
    self.location = loc.text
# Get Observation time
for tim in tree.findall(".//observation_time"):
    self.obtime = tim.text
# Get Current conditions
for weather in tree.findall(".//weather"):
    self.we = weather.text
# Get Temp
for TempF in tree.findall(".//temperature_string"):
    self.tmpB = TempF.text
#Get Humidity
for hum in tree.findall(".//relative_humidity"):
    self.relhum = hum.text
# Get Wind info
for windstring in tree.findall(".//wind_string"):
    self.winds = windstring.text
# Get Barometric Pressure
for pressure in tree.findall(".//pressure_string"):
    self.baroB = pressure.text
```

That's the end of the getCurrents function. Now we will work on the output function.

The Output Function

This simply prints the information that we have pulled from the XML file into a "human friendly" format in the terminal window:

```python
def output(self):
    print 'Weather Information From Wunderground.com'
    print 'Weather info for %s ' % self.location
    print self.obtime
    print 'Current Weather - %s' % self.we
    print 'Current Temp - %s' % self.tmpB
    print 'Barometric Pressure - %s' % self.baroB
    print 'Relative Humidity - %s' % self.relhum
    print 'Winds %s' % self.winds
```

The DoIt function accepts one parameter, the location Zip code. It then calls the getCurrents function with (in the code below) the debug mode turned off and the location. Then it calls the output function:

```
def DoIt(self,Location):
    self.getCurrents(0,Location)
    self.output()
```

That ends our class. It was very simple, but gives you a good idea how easily a class can be created.

The Main Function

The next bit of code is the main function. Again, it doesn't do very much for this particular program, but it gives a starting point for our program. The first line will assign the Zip code to the location variable. The second line will create an instance of our class. If it had an __init__ function, that would be called automatically when the class instance is created. Finally we call the DoIt function to start the whole thing off:

```
def main():
    location = '80013'
    currents = CurrentInfo()
    currents.DoIt(location)
```

Add the Program Entry Point

The last thing we will do is add the program entry point. We use the two lines starting with if __name__ and ending with main(). There are two built-in variables that Python handles for us. The first is __name__ (that's two underscore characters, the word 'name', and two more underscore characters). The other is just like the one we just described but is __main__ (again two underscores, the word 'main', and two more underscores). When you start a Python program from the command line, the __name__ variable is set by Python to __main__, so the interpreter knows that it is supposed to call the main() function. However, because we created a class that does all the work, we can actually treat this as a library and import the CurrentInfo class into another program. In that case, the main() function will not be run, because __name__ will not be __main__ but the name of the program calling it.

```
#=============================================================
# Main loop
#=============================================================
if __name__ == "__main__":
    main()
```

117

The output from our program class is as follows:

```
Weather Information From Wunderground.com
Weather info for Aurora, Colorado
Last Updated on November 14, 12:55 PM MST
Current Weather - Partly Cloudy
Current Temp - 54 F (12 C)
Barometric Pressure - 29.86 in (1011 mb)
Relative Humidity - 41%
Winds From the SSW at 5 MPH
```

As an aside, I have tested the source code by changing the location variable data from '80013' to 'W11 2BQ'. Everything worked as expected.

Index

A

Arithmetic operators, 13
Assignment operator, 17

B

Bitwise operator, 20
break statement, 46

C

Classes
    Bark function, 110
    Beagle object, 110–111
    class definition, 107
    CurrentConditions, 115
    CurrentInfo, 114
    debuglevel, 114
    Eat function, 109
    exit routine, 115
    getCurrents function, 114–116
    information reviewing, 112–113
    initialization function, 110
    libraries importing, 114
    location, 114
    main function, 117
    object, 107
    output function, 116
    Program Entry Point, 117–118
    self keyword, 109
    sleep function, 110
    Time to Code, 114
    try/except error, 115
    WeatherUnderground
        website, 112
    XML Refresher, 113–114

Conditional statements
    break statement, 46
    continue optional statement, 47
    else statement, 47
    for loop, 44–46
    IF/ELIF/ELSE statements, 43–44
    pass statement, 47
    while loop, 48

D

Data structures
    ColorList variable, 49
    dictionary
        blank dictionary, 56
        .clear() method, 57
        .copy() method, 57
        dict(list) function, 57
        .get(key[,default]) method, 57
        .has_key(key) method, 58
        information, 55
        .items() method, 58
        .iteritems() function, 56
        .keys() method, 58–59
        len(dictionary) function, 56
        .pop(key[,default]), 59
        .setdefault(key[,default]), 59
        update(other) method, 59
        .values() method, 60
    digging, 49
    list functions
        array, 50
        del(L[x]), 53
        for loop, 50
        L1 + L2, 52
        len(L) functions, 51
        L[x1\:x2], 52

▓ E

▓ F, G, H

▓ I, J

▓ K

▓ V, W, X, Y, Z

Get the eBook for only $10!

Now you can take the weightless companion with you anywhere, anytime. Your purchase of this book entitles you to 3 electronic versions for only $10.

This Apress title will prove so indispensible that you'll want to carry it with you everywhere, which is why we are offering the eBook in 3 formats for only $10 if you have already purchased the print book.

Convenient and fully searchable, the PDF version enables you to easily find and copy code—or perform examples by quickly toggling between instructions and   applications. The MOBI format is ideal for your Kindle, while the ePUB can be utilized on a variety of mobile devices.

Go to www.apress.com/promo/tendollars to purchase your companion eBook.